ONE BIG COUNTRY

A Big Book for the Union
Volume 1

Alistair McConnachie

ONE BIG COUNTRY

ONE BIG COUNTRY

To my Mother and Father.

Cover: Union Jacks at The Kelpies. A Force For Good welcomed Her Majesty when she opened the Queen Elizabeth II canal on 5 July 2017.

Copyright © 2023 Alistair McConnachie

Contents

INTRODUCTION

Let's get our fundamental philosophy and terminology straight before we begin.

Britain – is our shorthand for the entire United Kingdom of Great Britain and Northern Ireland. In this book, we will sometimes use the terms "Britain" and "UK" interchangeably for the purpose of rhetorical effectiveness.

Britain is a Unitary State – "a sovereign state governed as a single entity in which the central government is the supreme authority." (Wikipedia) Devolution has not changed this fact. Political misunderstanding about devolution has led to confusion – which we examine.

Britain is a Nation – Scottish nationalists disagree, and so do some "unionists". They see it as a conditional arrangement between 4 separate and distinct nations who, for the time being, choose to stay in Union, because it happens to suit their purposes.

We see Britain as much more substantial – as a Nation in itself.

Together, we are One Big Country – an additional creation of our parts, which have been coming together since the parliamentary union of Great Britain and Ireland on 1 January 1801; and the parliamentary union of Scotland and England on 1 May 1707; and the regal union of 24 March 1603; and the England and Wales union of 14 April 1536; and the social and cultural unions which have been developing since the dawn of time.

This means we are not so much a "union of nations" but a **Nation of Unions**.

We are bound together by economic necessity, but also by natural affinity – by our sense of shared identity and shared endeavour with our families throughout these Islands.

This means we are not so much a "family of nations" but a **Nation of Families**.

Britain has all the Evidence of Nationhood – we have a common Head of State, Parliament, political system of representative parliamentary democracy, international boundary, citizenship, language, currency, passport, anthem, flag, armed forces, seat on international bodies, and worldwide British Embassies. Even civil law is integrated, with the Supreme Court being the highest court for all UK civil cases.

Britain is definitely a Nation!

The on-going aim of staying together requires us to think of ourselves as one nation, with a shared identity, with more in common than what divides us, as greater than the sum of our parts, with a destiny to be together, to do more together, and to do more together than apart.

Our work at **A Force For Good** is about bringing Britain together!

It is about putting the sense of us being One Big Country – with a shared identity and destiny – first and foremost in our political decisions.

We proceed on that basis.

ONE BIG COUNTRY

PART 1

WE LOVE OUR ONE BIG COUNTRY

CHAPTER 1

ONE BIG COUNTRY: FUNDAMENTALS

The British Union is the political Union of Scotland, England, Northern Ireland and Wales, united in one Unitary State, with a sovereign national "Union Parliament".

The British Union is what holds Britain together. Our One Big Country is *built* upon the British Union. If it were not for the British Union then Britain would not exist politically; it would be a geographical term only.

It is not possible to be "for Britain" and against the British Union. If you care about Britain then you care about the British Union.

The political ideology upholding the British Union is called **Unionism.**

Britain is a direct *creation* of the ideology of Unionism. It is a direct *consequence* of Unionism.

Unionism is the political ideology which sustains the idea of Britain in the first place.

If you believe in Unionism – the fundamental political ideology which creates, underpins and maintains the British Union – then you believe in Britain. If you believe in Britain, then you believe in Unionism!

DEFINING UNIONISM: The Ideology underpinning Britain

We say all this because it's important to define **the foundational political ideology of Britain itself!** It's important to list **a set of characteristics** which describe our pro-UK belief; which describe "Unionism". Otherwise people won't know what we're talking about.

We must do this because *describing* one's political ideology *briefly* and in a manner which is *immediately understandable*, and which people can *remember* and *explain easily* to others, is a necessary requirement for the success of any political ideology.

After all, when people say they "believe in Scottish independence" everyone knows what they're talking about. They're talking about Scotland breaking away, mainly from England but ultimately from all parts of the British Isles.

That easy understanding is a big strength. It's one of the reasons why the political ideology of

Scottish independence has such traction. It is simple to describe, understand, remember and explain.

What should we – those of us who do not believe in Scottish independence – say in response?

If Scottish Independence is the belief in an independent Scotland and separate independent nations in the British Isles, then Unionism is the opposite. **It is the belief in a politically united British Isles.**

We can say: "I don't believe in Scottish independence – which is about Scotland being separated from the rest of the British Isles; I believe in unionism – which is about Scotland being united with the rest of the British Isles."

We can call it "Unionism" or "Scottish Unionism" or "British Unionism" or "pro-UK" or "pro-British" depending upon which term is the most relevant and effective in the conversation.

It is the core political ideology which creates, underpins and maintains the British Union and which binds together our **One Big Country**.

So it is high time it was properly acknowledged. It's high time we listed its characteristics, as follows!

12 BRITISH UNIONIST FUNDAMENTALS

1. Britain is a Nation in its own right, and not just a political State. The social, cultural, regal and political Unions created it into a Nation, and into our One Big Country. (Some Scottish nationalists will immediately dispute this because they know it is central to our belief. By doing so, they demonstrate an intolerance to the basis of our allegiance and identity.)

2. Britain is our country, as much as Scotland is our country, and we do not want to see it broken up.

3. We have more in common than what divides us, and it makes sense for our political institutions to reflect that fact.

4. We stand for the values of solidarity not separation, of unity not division, of giving not getting, of all for one and one for all.

5. Britain united is greater than the sum of its parts.

6. The constituent parts of Britain are related as in a family; which means that it's not appropriate for one part to put itself first without due regard to the other members. We do not put any part of Britain before the common good of all.

7. A problem in any part of Britain concerns us all, and the challenges which confront us throughout these Islands are most effectively resolved by working together.

8. Scotland within a united Britain is a better place to live, socially and economically, and with greater opportunity for all, than a Scotland separated.

9. Scotland within a united Britain makes global strategic and diplomatic sense, and is more influential internationally, than a Scotland separated.

10. Britain is the best Nation within which to accommodate diverse identities. It's big enough to allow for English, Irish, Scottish and Welsh identities, and all the variations within them, to rub along and exist together. This does not work the other way, as Ireland has demonstrated. When you take fish out the big British pond and put them in a bowl, then the differences in the bowl are amplified.

11. Britain is an evolving organism tending naturally towards unity, not spinning out of control towards separation.

12. Britain is a Work in Progress. There wasn't any time – ever since Britain "first arose from out the Azure Main" – when we could say, "This was the perfect Union. This was the perfect Britain." It is something that we are always building together. It is an ideal we seek and work towards. It is our Great Work of Time! **Each day, we write a page in our endless story.**

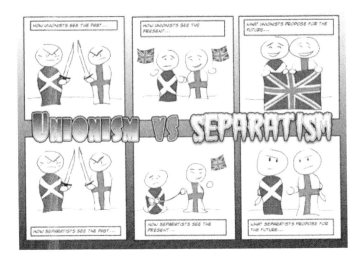

Further Reading

We developed the practical idea of the British Union in depth in our Speech in London (24-6-15), "One UK: The British Union from 30 First Principles" on our Legacy Site at http://www.aforceforgood.org.uk/strategy/firstprins/

We no longer publish on our Legacy Site **aForceForGood.org.uk** but it remains online as a vital resource for authentic Unionism and a valuable record of this period in British history. Please note, it is a "http" site and not a "https" site. If you use the latter "s" protocol, then it won't open correctly. Since 1 May 2018 we publish at **aForceForGood.UK**

CHAPTER 2

THE UNITED KINGDOM: OUR ONE BIG COUNTRY

The United Kingdom is our One Big Country and we don't want to see it broken up. The UK is our Big British Home, from which it makes no sense to deliberately downsize.

We don't see Scotland, England, Wales and Northern Ireland as separate houses which belong to our "neighbours".

For us, the entire United Kingdom is our Home, and the people within it are our Family.

They are all parts of our Home which belong to **our Family**.

Scottish nationalists look puzzlingly on us and say, "Why would you not want your nation to be independent?"; without realising that we see

Scotland as our nation within our bigger nation, the United Kingdom.

We see Scotland as a great nation, which becomes even greater, within Great Britain.

We see Scotland as an intrinsic part of the overall creation, whose separation from it would endanger the entire Living Organism.

This is a fundamentally different way of looking at things from the Scottish nationalist way of looking at things.

They understand the UK only as a political state, a temporary political arrangement, to which Scotland is hitched.

For our part, we understand the UK philosophically, and we experience the UK physically, not only as a state, but also as a nation, with an identity, which benefits us.

Here is an example of how our approach differs from the nationalist approach.

In a newspaper article, prior to the 2014 UK membership referendum (*Scotland on Sunday*, 5-4-14), written by the then leader of the Welsh nationalist party, Plaid Cymru, she addressed her Scottish readership in the first sentence, saying, "All of a sudden, outsiders have started taking an interest in your country."

"Your country"; as if she and we are foreigners to each other! Throughout the article she spoke about Scotland as "you" and "yours". And then talked about Wales as "my country".

That kind of exclusionary language is completely opposite to the sort of language which we pro-UK people use. It is not how we understand the relationship at all.

We don't look on Wales, or England, or Northern Ireland and talk about "you" or "yours".

We look on all these countries and we talk about "we", about "our", about "us".

That's because we recognise that we are all part of the same bigger country, the United Kingdom.

Within the UK, Scotland is not just "our" country. It is her country too! And for our part, Wales is also our country. It is not only "her" country.

And that's a truly great thing, and it helps to explain why Scotland, England, Northern Ireland and Wales are not actually the "normal" countries that the nationalists might try to pretend.

We are all unique countries involved in a unique relationship. And together we make up an even more unique country, the United Kingdom; which we have all helped to build.

An amazing, fascinating, successful **One Big Country**.

Understanding the United Kingdom as our Home and our Family is powerful *physically* too.

We experience the feeling and we enjoy the benefits of it in our day to day lives.

For example, we can go for a weekend to Newcastle knowing that when we're there, we are still in our own country. We can take the ferry to Belfast, and enjoy the friendship of our fellow countrymen and women. We can go to Wales on holiday knowing that when we're there, we're still in our own country.

And it is good that someone from England can come up to Scotland knowing that when he or she is here, they are still in their own country.

You know, somebody from England doesn't need to be told to "go home" to their "own country." They are already home; they are already in their own country: the United Kingdom.

That is a very inclusive way to understand our relationship. In action it is a powerful and enriching experience. We can be four Countries but we are One Big Country also. We can be four Teams but we can be One Big Team also. So let's continue to play for the UK Team. Because we love being part of it. We don't want to see everything breaking up.

Thankfully, we did not wake up on the 19 September 2014, the day after the referendum, and discover that we had lost *two thirds of our country*; two thirds of our Home. We did not wake up and realise that we had lost 90% of our fellow citizens; 90% of our Family! (1)

And if you're from England, Northern Ireland, or Wales, you don't want to wake up one day and find out that you've lost one third of your Home and ten percent of your Family.

So let's Stay Together with the UK.

Let's not downsize from our Big British Home because being part of the UK gives us all One Big Country to call our own.

1. According to Wikipedia (downloaded 12-5-14) the population of the UK on that date was 63,705,000 and the population of Scotland was 5,327,700 (which is 8.4%). The land mass of the UK is 94,060 sq mi and that of Scotland is 30,414 sq mi (32.3%).

Alistair McConnachie with Union Flag overlooking Loch Lomond. Painting by M McConnachie.

CHAPTER 3

REASONS TO LOVE THE GREAT BRITISH UNION

On Saturday 1st May 2021, A Force For Good held its "1st May, Great British Union Day" celebration in George Square, Glasgow. We celebrated the Birthday of the United Kingdom while on the other side of the Square, a Scottish nationalist group were agitating to destroy it! AFFG Founder, Alistair McConnachie gave two Speeches. The second one, based on the following text, described some benefits of Union today and looked with enthusiasm to the opportunity that our shared future will bring.

We're Scottish and we're British. We love the UK, and we will Stay Together!

You know, some of the people on the other side of the Square will ask "What is the point of the United Kingdom? What is the point of the Union?"

Well, let's tell them. Let's give them a positive message about the United Kingdom, about our **Nation of Unions** through time, which has created today our **Nation of Families**.

The purpose of the Union – the purpose of *any* Union – is to make it possible to enjoy the benefits which come from working together.

What are some of those benefits today which the Union enables us to enjoy? They are economic, social, cultural, political.

ECONOMIC BENEFITS

Economically, the point of the Union is to pool and share our resources to help our closest neighbours and family members when they are in need; and to be helped by them, when we are in need!

We don't mind sharing. We are all about giving, not getting. Sometimes we give more than we get back. Sometimes we get back more than we give. That's the nature of living in a Union.

But we know this: We know that Scotland is big enough, and rich enough, and clever enough to share its resources and its wealth with its family members throughout these Islands. Indeed, it is a source of great pride to us that we do so!

It is obvious that Scotland is better protected economically as part of a larger monetary Union. It was true in 1707 and it is true today.

We only need look at the billions of pounds which come to Scotland from the British Treasury.

Any call for separation can only be made by completely ignoring this economic reality; an economic reality which proves that, in times of crisis, we are stronger together.

In times of crisis, **the Union is the best insurance policy ever devised**.

You know, it is important to emphasise the clear economic benefits, and the absolute danger of mega-levels of austerity which would occur under a separated Scotland.

But of course, the Union is much more than economic!

OUR DUAL IDENTITY – Scottish and British
The Union of 1707 created a new Nation, in addition to Scotland and England and Wales – a new Nation which allowed us to claim all parts of this Island as our own.

Today, this enables us to enjoy the benefits of a dual identity; being both Scottish and British without having to choose between one or the other.

And that freedom – to be both Scottish and British – is another positive benefit of the Union of the United Kingdom.

It's a very valuable social and cultural possession which enables us to be part of the wider community of these Islands, to fit in, and to enjoy the benefits which come from that shared identity.

It means that people in Scotland can look upon Northern Ireland, Wales and England, as belonging to us too, because we are all part of our One Big Country.

And people from Northern Ireland, Wales and England can look upon Scotland as part of their country too – all of us united by our British identity, in one Kingdom, which belongs to us all.

You know, Scottish nationalists want to narrow our sense of identity to "Scottish only". They want us to choose between being one or the other.

But the Union has ensured that we don't have to choose. We can be both Scottish and British.

What a wonderful fact!

As pro-UK people, we are about encouraging everyone to enjoy that shared sense of identity.

We encourage people in Scotland to enjoy and appreciate, **as their own**, the culture and the achievements of all the people in all the other parts of the United Kingdom. And we encourage people in the rest of the UK to look upon what we offer in Scotland, as their birthright also.

If you understand yourself as British, then it all belongs to you. All of it! Immense benefits flow from that shared identity.

And we say to the Scottish nationalists – if you want it, it's there for you too!

So the Union offers us that very useful dual identity. It offers **the best of both worlds**.

A separate Scotland would, inevitably, make it harder to be British and would ultimately remove the choice. Sadly, we've seen how that operates in the Republic of Ireland.

POLITICAL BENEFITS OF UNION

Politically, a good way to demonstrate what we have here in the United Kingdom, is to contrast the UK with the EU.

You know, many Scottish nationalists love the EU more than they love the rest of the UK. It seems strange?

They want to throw away our centuries old Union – and turn their backs, not only on the rest of the UK, which is Scotland's biggest trading area, but on the very people who are often their closest family – and for what?

It is especially ridiculous because the United Kingdom represents the very thing that the European Union *aspires* to be. Think about it.

Here's an excerpt from an article which describes how the political benefits we have in the UK – and which have been built up over the centuries – is what the EU would love to have, if only it could!

Here are some essential ingredients for a successful, sovereign multinational union: an effective single currency covering a highly integrated economic area, along with fiscal risk-sharing and wealth redistribution across that area (such as the Barnett formula governing public spending in Scotland, Wales and Northern Ireland). A comprehensive single market in goods and services is also a key requirement. Then you need a single, risk-free sovereign debt market; a banking union; a united foreign, security and defence policy; deep cultural and family ties; shared values; unlimited, uncontentious free movement of people; representative institutions with real power and (usually) popular legitimacy; a shared head of state; and similar legal traditions. A shared mother tongue is useful, too. (1)

All of these things we have in the UK. All of these things we already enjoy politically. The UK provides all of these things for Scotland – ready-made!

But still the SNP and the Greens want to break away from those things.

The fact is, if Scotland were already separate, we would want to re-create a United Kingdom for all the political benefits of association which come from being in Union. That doesn't mean that we won't criticise Westminster, and our

MPs, when it's necessary. Of course we will, and we should. There is often much to criticise. But that's the case with any political system.

THE BOTTOM LINE – We have more in Common than what Divides us!
What does it come down to?

Ultimately, the Union is a recognition that the people of the United Kingdom have more in common than what divides us, and so our political institutions should reflect that fact.

That's how we see things.

Unfortunately, the Scottish nationalists believe that we have more that *divides us*, than what we have in common.

LOOKING FORWARD to a NEW AGE of GRAND ACHIEVEMENT
So as we go forward, we understand our United Kingdom as One Big Country, not just 4 separate and squabbling ones.

One Big Country in which we are privileged to enjoy a shared identity, enabling us to be both Scottish and British, and to enjoy as our own all the political, economic, social and cultural benefits which come from that intimate connection.

Let us understand the United Kingdom as having come together through time, to the point where, today, we are literally a **Nation of Families** much more than a "family of separate nations".

Above all, it is our Home – all of it – and we don't want to see our Home broken up!

We know that since, at least, the Union of Crowns in 1603, and certainly since the Union in 1707, the Scots have been at the centre of Britain's achievements on the world stage. And that is where we should be. That is where we must remain.

Our place is at the centre, leading, or – if you prefer – disproportionately contributing to, the success of the United Kingdom.

That's the positive place to be – helping Britain to a new level of accomplishment on the world stage, to a new age of Grand Achievement.

For the Union presents to us – as it has always done – **the Great Opport*unity*.**

The Union is an idea and like all ideas it is constantly being tested. It is for those of us who believe in it, to keep it alive in our minds, in our hearts and souls, and in our physical reality. **That's what we at A Force For Good work to do.**

Believe us when we say, the men and women of A Force For Good will stay the course for the Union we so love!

God Bless the United Kingdom and God Save the King!

1. Alex Carew, "How Brexit will save the United Kingdom", *Money Week*, 25-7-19 at moneyweek.com/511743/how-brexit-will-save-the-united-kingdom

A Force For Good's "Great British Union Day" Rally,
George Square, Glasgow, 1-5-21.

CHAPTER 4

IF YOU'RE BRITISH, YOU'RE INVOLVED!

The deliberate exclusion of the wider British voice leads to restricted debate, an inaccurate ballot paper, and the repudiation of the role of the British Parliament. This must change because we're all involved in keeping the UK together!

During the 2014 referendum, the SNP set the bounds of the debate. Not only did they get to choose the date and length of the campaign, the franchise (including 16 year olds and EU citizens), the question, the answers, and the words on the ballot paper itself; but they also managed to ensure that people from outside Scotland were excluded from the debate, and felt awkward about joining.

They successfully "de-legitimised" voices from the rest of the UK.

This meant that people from outside Scotland were reluctant to voice an opinion, even though it was about the future of their own One Big Country – the United Kingdom!

We realised there was a problem when a woman who lived in Scotland said to us, "I'm from England so maybe I shouldn't have an opinion on this."

We told her immediately, "If you're British, you're involved!"

It made us realise that everyone should be welcome and encouraged to participate in the debate to keep our shared Nation together.

Never again can we allow the de-legitimisation of British voices from outside Scotland.

This is not just about Scotland "becoming independent". It's primarily about breaking up the United Kingdom itself, and it is absurd that less than 4% of the entire British electorate could be responsible for such a catastrophe (see chapter 8).

Everyone has to be engaged and involved.

EVEN the BALLOT PAPER EXCLUDED the REST of the UK

The SNP's exclusion of the rest of the United Kingdom even extended to the way the question was framed and the way the ballot paper itself was written. Compare these 2 examples.

On the 2014 ballot paper, the United Kingdom was not mentioned. It was entirely ignored. It was as if the little matter of "the United Kingdom" was somehow not relevant to the matter at hand.

Compare this with the ballot paper for the 2016 referendum on EU membership where the EU was mentioned 5 times!

The heading on the EU Referendum ballot paper read, "Referendum on the United Kingdom's membership of the European Union". The question read "Should the United Kingdom remain a member of the European Union or leave the European Union?" The answers given were, "Remain a member of the European Union" and "Leave the European Union".

It was all about the European Union!

However, the referendum on whether Scotland should leave or remain in the United Kingdom appeared to have nothing to do with the United Kingdom on the ballot paper, or in the question!

That cannot be allowed again. And please do not think that is of no significance.

The fact is, we went into the Voting Booth in 2014 and we were presented with a piece of paper which made no mention of the United Kingdom, the very thing we were trying to keep together and prevent being broken apart.

That was undoubtedly worth percentage points to the separatists.

Even the way we consequently speak of the 2 referendums has been forged by these different emphases. For example, many of us will speak of the "2014 Scottish independence" referendum, and the "2016 EU membership" referendum.

We don't normally speak about the "2014 UK membership" referendum, or the "2016 UK independence" referendum, and that is a direct consequence of the way the matters were successfully framed by the SNP and the mainstream media.

THE SURVIVAL of the UNITED KINGDOM CONCERNS US ALL!

This point was raised very well by only a handful of journalists during the run up to the 2014 referendum. For example, Fiona Laird wrote:

I have always considered myself British. But if Britain is about to be redefined as a country that doesn't include Scotland, then I don't feel British at all. Living in a country that has Scotland as part of it is an essential part of who I am. Over the last few months, I have realised I have very strong feelings about all this – but it seems there is no approved outlet for them.

I am supposed to just sit here and take whatever happens in the referendum without saying a word. It feels like being left by a lover

I have lived with for years and not being allowed to make any contribution to the discussion about our future...

Speaking of the pro-UK campaign, she said:

> It needs to do something fast to prove that the UK population feels much as it does about the current government, the status quo and the future. This isn't a fight between Scots and English; that's an invention of the yes campaign. Better Together needs Welsh voices on board, and Geordies, Liverpudlians and Mancunians. The 'rest of the UK' is so much more than a few smug Londoners, despite what the yes campaign would have us believe. (1)

Jenny McCartney put it well:

> One of the most seductive things about the UK is that you can travel anywhere in it – from Land's End to John O'Groats to the rugged Antrim Coast – and be aware that, although perhaps a stranger to locals, you are not a foreigner: at some fundamental level, its curiosities and beauties belong to all of us. That's a deep, unspoken kind of magic, and I wonder how many people have considered what it would feel like if it disappeared. If

Scotland becomes an independent country, it would officially render me a foreigner to it, an automatic outsider, a tolerated guest. It's not a feeling I yearn for. (2)

As we've already said, we at A Force For Good believe that it's great to visit, or go on holiday, or work in another part of Britain and say, "This is my country too". Those who identify only with one part of our Islands, don't have that psychological feeling, and can't share that joy.

Scotland and England are uniquely blessed by the fact that we are also part of the same country – the United Kingdom. We here in Scotland don't want to have to look on England as a foreign country!

Graeme Archer spoke about the "poetry of the Union" and our shared togetherness:

The poetry of the Union is simple, but provides the strongest reason to oppose Salmond's carve-up-a-small-island nationalism: that I was born in Scotland to an English father and Scottish mother, and now live in London. That's it. But this one sentence contains the big question that separatists prefer to avoid. Namely, why should my parents be made foreigners to one another, and I to one of them? (3)

TRYING to EXCLUDE the LEGITIMATE ROLE of the BRITISH PARLIAMENT

The belief that nobody should have a say except people in Scotland, also leads the SNP and its supporters to say that the decision to have another referendum is for people "in Scotland alone". This leads them to claim that the British Parliament has no right to prevent one.

This is because they frame the matter as Scotland "becoming independent".

In contrast, we see this as about keeping the UK together. We see it as about not breaking up, and about making it even greater than it is.

And those are matters for all the people of the UK who want to stay together.

HOW WE ARE ALL INVOLVED

We are all involved, firstly, through our MPs in the British Parliament – where our representatives have the ultimate say on whether there should be a referendum; and secondly through our own actions, such as helping those who are trying to keep the UK together, through physical, financial, and moral support (see chapter 19).

To conclude, the matter of Scottish separation is not for Scotland alone because this is not about Scotland alone.

This is about keeping Britain together.

And keeping Britain together is a matter for all of us who believe in Britain, wherever we live in our Islands, or indeed the world. As we always say, "If you're British, you're involved".

And even if you're not British, but you like the idea of the United Kingdom, then you're involved too!

1. Fiona Laird, "I'm British, and I want to be able to talk about Scotland's independence vote", *The Guardian*, online 29-4-14, tinyurl.com/427pxj8m

2. Jenny McCartney, "Scottish independence: There's a kind of magic in our united kingdom", *The Sunday Telegraph*, 1-12-13, tinyurl.com/bdhbs5d6

3. Graeme Archer, "If Scotland kills off the Union, I will be an immigrant in my own country", *The Daily Telegraph*, 7-2-14, tinyurl.com/2fyymtup

PART 2

UNDERSTANDING DEVOLUTION

ONE BIG COUNTRY

CHAPTER 5

OUR UNITARY STATE

*Despite what the SNP says, devolved institutions are British institutions and are intended to be part of our wider political unity. Yet it is clear that most MPs and MSPs, of all parties, do not properly understand the **purpose** of devolution nor the actual **constitutional basis** upon which it is founded, and the subsequent **relationship** between the British Parliament and its devolved arms. This chapter explains all these things.*

THE PURPOSE of DEVOLUTION
Without making a judgement on whether it is a good or bad idea, the intended purpose is to compensate for the minority representation of MPs from Scotland, Northern Ireland and Wales, in

relation to those from England, in the collective British Parliament.

For example, at the 2019 General Election, the number of MPs from England was 533 out of 650, Scotland had 59, Wales 40 and Northern Ireland 18. Some Scottish nationalists complain that all the MPs in England could outvote Scotland, Wales, and Northern Ireland together, by over 4 and a half times. (1)

However, **this never happens** because MPs vote on party and ideological lines. They do not vote on national lines. That is, Parliament votes on Tory v Labour v Lib Dem v SNP v DUP v Plaid v Other lines. Parties can also split as a result of ideological difference, and Tories can vote against Tories, Labour against Labour, and so on.

So, the reality is that Scotland never gets "outvoted" because no countries get outvoted. There is never an "England versus Scotland" split! It is political parties, and ideological tendencies which get outvoted at Westminster.

Scottish nationalists have always been fixated on this mythical "England versus Scotland" voting split – which never happens – because they like to think that the SNP *is* Scotland. So when the SNP gets outvoted, they see it as "Scotland" being outvoted! Union-minded people don't think of the British Parliament in this "country versus country" way. **Our ideal is that all the MPs consider, and**

vote for, the best interests of all the United Kingdom taken together as one.

Nevertheless, to the extent that this became an issue – due to the rise of Scottish nationalism – then **devolution was intended to compensate for this imbalance of numbers by giving Scotland control over certain powers which could be exercised at the Scotland level, without it causing problems for the wider UK.**

This is also why England does not have "a devolved English Parliament". Nobody was suggesting it at the time because the whole point of devolution was meant to be to compensate for the imbalance in MP numbers when contrasted with the total number of MPs in England.

The idea of devolution might have made more sense were it not for the fact that Scotland already had a very vocal separatist movement!

At the time of the devolution referendum on 11 September 1997, many of us feared that if a platform were built for the SNP to exploit, then it would only be a matter of time before they came to dominate it, and use it against the Union Parliament.

That is, of course, exactly what happened in 2007, and it only took 3 elections!

Devolution might work "to strengthen the Union" in the absence of separatist movements, but it can be dangerous to the integrity of the State in the presence of these movements.

So that was the intended *purpose* of devolution. Let's look at how it is intended *to work* in practice.

This requires us first to understand **the constitutional basis** of the United Kingdom, so we can then understand how the devolved powers **relate outwards** from the centre.

THE CONSTITUTIONAL BASIS: The UK is a UNITARY STATE

That is, the UK is "a sovereign state governed as a single entity in which the central government is the supreme authority." This is the definition of "Unitary State" on Wikipedia.

The Scottish "government", under the SNP and Green administration, do not want to believe that the UK is a Unitary State. They get their civil servants – who work for the British Home Civil Service – to write papers which **entirely misrepresent the actual constitutional basis and relationship**, and which tell us that Scotland is not part of a Unitary State.

See for example, the statement that Scotland is "not a region of a unitary state" on a July 2022 report which was written by British civil servants who have been co-opted by the SNP and Green coalition to promote their anti-UK agenda. (2)

By suggesting that the UK does not have the cohesion and constitutional integrity of a Unitary State – but is somehow just a loose association of different nations who are putting up with each other for the time being, and just for as long as it suits their purposes – then the SNP and Greens are deliberately misrepresenting the constitutional relationship as conditional (meaning, dependent upon various conditions being met; not a fixed and absolute thing).

This creates a very weak and fragile constitutional relationship. It suggests that the ties that bind are frayed; that the relationship is constantly to be called into question, and undermined, and made unstable. This makes it much easier to break up.

Understanding the relationship as conditional makes it easier to promote a divisive, separatist agenda.

On the other hand, **understanding the UK as a Unitary State – which is fixed – helps contribute to its cohesion and permanence.**

THE DEVOLUTIONARY RELATIONSHIP with the BRITISH PARLIAMENT

Following on from the fact that we are literally a Unitary State, then **devolution is best understood as British State Power exercised by Subsidiary Arms of the British Political Body.**

Holyrood, Cardiff and Stormont are **Arms** of the British Political **Body**. They are intimately connected with, and intended to be used for, the overall health and assistance of the British Body.

In this way, Holyrood is properly understood as a British institution in Scotland, which is exercising powers which have flowed from the central, collective British Parliament at Westminster which, in itself, represents every single person, and all parts, in our United Kingdom.

Holyrood is in a vertical not horizontal relationship with the central British Parliament; it is in a hierarchical, not level, relationship. It is not on an equivalent plane of political power. It is not "equal and opposite"; but rather it is a functioning organ of the British State itself.

The subsidiary bodies exercise certain powers, but the relationship requires them to defer to the central British Parliament when necessary.

That's the theory at least. That's what devolution is meant to be about. Indeed, we were told that "devolution would strengthen the Union".

That may have been the intention, but once devolution was established, there was little thought given to the practice, and to the danger of such institutions being captured by separatist movements.

There was little done to embed Holyrood intimately with the British Parliament.

Almost from the start, and certainly after the SNP arrived in 2007 to exploit the lack of understanding, there has been a fiction that Holyrood is some kind of quasi-independent body existing on an equivalent level, and in natural opposition, to the central British State.

Today, the SNP seek to portray Holyrood as an opponent to the British Parliament, on the same plane of political power; as some kind of "subjugated equivalent". It will not accept that it is more properly understood as an arm of the British Parliamentary governing structure in Scotland.

WE NEED to CHANGE "THE DEVOLUTION SETTLEMENT"

The phrase "devolution settlement" actually means the particular **Model** of devolution used for Holyrood.

When it was established, the British Government produced the worst kind of devolution Model – a Reserved Powers Model. That means: Everything is devolved to the administrative unit (Holyrood) except that which is specifically written down as reserved to the central British Parliament.

The reserved stuff is written down specifically, and absolutely everything else is considered devolved. The presumption is that everything is devolved unless stated in writing otherwise.

This includes the devolution of things which have been forgotten about, things not known about yet, and things which the SNP decides to do because it's not been written down as reserved.

An example of the latter is changing the name of the Scottish Executive to "Scottish Government". Another example is the Travel Ban to Manchester. (3) The SNP just did it, and waited for the British Government to challenge them (which it never did).

It is an unstable Model because the extent of the devolved power has not been limited to that which is specifically written down and known. It has been left wide open and free to expand by itself, even into areas not even known about at the time the devolved legislation was drafted. It's like an unstable gas, constantly trying to expand and embrace new areas of power, to the detriment of the centre.

The Reserved Powers Model is "the wrong way round". It is this wrong-way-round "Devolution Settlement" which is the primary means by which the SNP continually expands its power and influence into areas in which it has no business, to the detriment of the Union.

The Right Way Round – the Conferred Powers Model

The proper Model, the only sensible and stable Model for devolution – if a central Unitary State is genuinely intent on maintaining its authority – is to use a "Conferred Powers" (sometimes called "Devolved Powers") Model.

A Conferred Powers Model means: Everything is reserved to the central British Parliament except that which is specifically written down as devolved (conferred) to the administrative unit (Holyrood).

The devolved stuff is written down specifically, and absolutely everything else is considered reserved. The presumption is that everything is reserved unless stated in writing otherwise.

That means the reserved stuff includes things which have been forgotten about, things not yet known about, and things which the devolved administration might want to make up.

This is the only Model which accurately reflects the true nature of a Unitary State; that is, a State which has one central, collective, national Parliament in which all powers are vested and from which all powers flow.

We need to reverse the current convention where matters not explicitly reserved are considered to be devolved. We need to establish a new convention where matters not explicitly devolved are considered to be reserved.

This is a crucial way for a Unitary State, such as the UK, to protect its integrity. We must change the "Devolution Settlement" from a Reserved Powers Model to a Conferred Powers Model.

1. At the 2024 General Election, the number of overall seats remains at 650, but England has been increased to 543, Scotland has been reduced to 57, Wales to 32, with Northern Ireland remaining at 18.

2. Scottish Government, "Renewing Democracy through Independence" at "Executive Summary", 14 July 2022 at tinyurl.com/49askvbz

In chapter 13 we show why the British Home Civil Service should not be co-opted on British Taxpayers' money to promote policies deliberately intended to destroy the British State itself.

3. See "SNP has no Legal Right to Restrict Travel in UK", 22-6-21 at aforceforgood.uk/single-post/no-right-to-stop-uk-travel

HOW DEVOLUTION IS MEANT TO WORK

A Unitary State with Subsidiary Arms intended to compensate for the Minority Representation of those Areas in the Collective British Parliament

British Parliament and Government

Northern Ireland Executive

Scottish Executive

Welsh Executive

Vertical Relationship with Executives

The number of MPs from England is 533 out of 650. Scottish Nationalists complain that all the MPs in England could outvote Scotland (59) Wales (40) and Northern Ireland (18) together, by over 4 and a half times. This never happens since MPs vote on party and ideological lines, not on national lines.

But to the extent that it became an issue (due to the rise of Scottish Nationalism) devolution was intended to compensate for the imbalance.

Devolution can only work though, if the devolved institutions are understood as Arms of the overall Collective British Parliamentary Body, which work in co-operation with that Parliament. It does not work when separatist parties, or parties which do not understand this unitary relationship, gain control of any of the devolved Arms and imagine that they are on an equivalent political level, and in opposition to, the Collective British Parliamentary Body.

When that happens, we end up with this....

HOW DEVOLUTION HAS ENDED UP!

Quasi-Federalism and Slow Independence

Horizontal Relationship with "Governments"

Scottish "Government"

Welsh "Government"

Actual British Government

Don't forget about me!

The relationship is <u>horizontal</u> and the separate "Governments" attempt to compete on equal terms with, and often in opposition to, the Collective British Parliament with no regard for the fact that it represents our unity. [*The NI Executive is not yet termed a "government".*] If the UK is to survive, we need to get back to understanding what devolution was meant to be. Also see: "The British Union from 30 First Principles at aforceforgood.org.uk/strategy/firstprins/

CHAPTER 6

HOLYROOD IS BRITISH!

Holyrood is a British institution. It was created by the British Parliament in order to help govern the British State. It's not an independent creation of a separate Scottish State, no matter how much the SNP and Greens might try to misrepresent it. As a devolved Arm of the overall British Body, it cannot destroy Britain. It cannot deliver a "mandate" to break us up.

Our previous chapter described how Holyrood is an intricate arm of the British parliament; an intrinsic organ.

For devolution to work – rather than just be a slippery slope to separation – the devolved institutions need to be understood and described as British institutions; institutions which are part of a wider political unity, symbolised by the British Parliament.

Ideally, the devolved institutions should be working together with this central Union Parliament, for the greater good of the entire UK, rather than at each other's throats to the detriment of national stability.

There needs to be more effort to understand, describe and label the devolved institutions firmly within this wider British political context.

UNDERSTANDING HOLYROOD as a BRITISH INSTITUTION is KEY

For example, on 17 January 2023 the British Government made a Section 35 order to prohibit the SNP/Green's "Gender Recognition Reform" Bill going to Royal Assent. Many people were extremely grateful that the Government had stepped in to prevent it being passed into law.

This intervention was entirely proper and consistent with the way devolution is meant to work in our constitutional democracy.

As a devolved Arm of the overall British Political Body, Holyrood is *ideally* meant to deliver policies at the Scottish level which don't conflict with the interests of the rest of the UK. Without this understanding, nothing makes sense!

If you do not understand Holyrood as a British institution connected intimately within the wider British Political Body – but instead you understand it as some kind of quasi-independent Parliament which is free to do its own thing regardless – then it is perfectly understandable that you will be confused when it gets overruled by the British Parliament.

If you wrongly imagine that the Scottish Parliament is an equal and opposite Parliament to Westminster, and if you wrongly imagine the administration at Holyrood to be an equal and opposite "Government" to the British Government, then of course, you are going to be upset when that British Parliament and Government overrules a Holyrood vote.

If you do not understand the correct constitutional relationship between the overall British Political Body and its devolved Arms then it is perfectly understandable that you might be angry if it is overruled. You might well call it "democracy being denied".

And we're not going to blame you for that misunderstanding!

Ever since Holyrood was established in 1999, the various British Governments have not properly clarified the relationship. They even go as far as to deliberately confuse the relationship by using constitutionally-muddled terms such as "our two Governments"!

As we explain in chapter 11, this leads to some Scottish nationalists thinking that Holyrood is some kind of "subjugated equivalent".

Why HOLYROOD CANNOT DELIVER a SEPARATION MANDATE

A serious consequence of this constitutionally-muddled rhetoric is that it has now encouraged people to believe that a Holyrood election is capable of delivering a "mandate" for separation.

After all, if you understand Holyrood as a quasi-independent Parliament which is somehow equal, opposite and apart from the British State which created it, then of course you will imagine that a mandate to break up the British State can be obtained at a Holyrood election.

However, if you understand it correctly as a British institution within the British State – if you understand that its purpose is, ideally, to ensure the Unitary British State can be governed in a more effective manner – then you will understand that it is not intended to deliver a mandate to break-up that Unitary British State, and it is not competent to do so.

Of course, when Holyrood was set up, there was no thought given to the possibility that the institution would be captured by people who wanted to destroy the British State.

There was no thought given to the possibility

that such people would reject the constitutional function of Holyrood as an integrated Arm of the wider British Body; which was intended to improve governance in Scotland; while respecting the wider UK political context.

There was no thought given to the possibility that such people would instead misrepresent it as a quasi-independent Parliament, equal and in perpetual opposition to the British centre; and that they would use it to try to destroy the wider UK.

Indeed, there was no thought given to very much at all!

EXPLAINING SECTION 35
So what can we do? Well, at least we can explain how things are meant to operate.

The Scotland Act 1998 set up Holyrood. Section 35 states:

> ***35. Power to intervene in certain cases***
> *(1) If a Bill contains provisions -*
> *(a) which the Secretary of State has reasonable grounds to believe would be incompatible with any international obligations or the interests of defence or national security, or*
> *(b) which make modifications of the law as it applies to reserved matters and which the Secretary of State has reasonable grounds to believe would have an adverse effect on the*

operation of the law as it applies to reserved matters,
he may make an order prohibiting the Presiding Officer from submitting the Bill for Royal Assent.

That's perfectly understandable. It makes clear that we don't live in a society where the devolved Arms can do what they want.

We live in a constitutional democracy, which means we have laws which stop devolved Arms passing bills which negatively affect the rest of the UK Body. **This is not "undermining devolution". This is how devolution is meant to work!**

Devolution cannot possibly work if policies in devolved areas are negatively impacting the rest of the UK.

Of course, the SNP and Greens understand all of this.

They are happy for their policies to negatively impact the rest of the UK. That's because they purposely do not want devolution to work. They want to make it unworkable within the UK, in order to more easily promote their divisive agenda.

Let's remind them, and all the other MPs and MSPs:
1. Devolution is not a blank policy slate for the devolved areas.
2. Devolution is not meant to allow devolved policies at the expense of the entire UK.

3. Devolution is not a Trojan Horse to be used against the integrity of the Union, and it's not a Battering Ram against the British Parliament and Government either.

The UK is a democracy, but we are more than that! We are a constitutional democracy – our political system runs via laws which aim to protect everyone in the UK – such as Section 35 of the Scotland Act.
      That means the British Government is always justified in stepping-in when a devolved Bill will harm the overall integrity of the United Kingdom.

DEVOLUTION is an ADDED PRIVILEGE
The Scottish nationalist grievance narrative is that the 1707 Parliamentary Union somehow took away Scotland's "freedom" and turned Scotland into a "colony" of England, and that devolution is Scotland breaking away from the Union in order for it to try to achieve some kind of perfected state of independence again.
      It's time to reframe that grievance narrative into a positive one!
      The reality is that at no point has anyone taken anything away from Scotland.
      The 1707 Union was the joining of two sovereign Kingdoms to create a new United Kingdom where the Kingdoms of Scotland and England (with Wales regarded as a Principality of

the Kingdom of England) were assimilated to each other as equals.

It was not the "subjugation" which some nationalists might pretend. Instead, the members of the Scottish Parliament became the members of the new British Parliament, just as the previous members of the English Parliament became members of the new Parliament also.

Then, in addition, by the end of the twentieth century, there was special consideration given to Scotland within the Union, as a result of the complaints which some people had about lack of representation – as examined in chapter 5.

As a result, there was an *adding* of special privilege to Scotland, via devolution.

You can't add this extra privilege and call it "colonisation" or "oppression", when it is quite the opposite!

Devolution is literally adding a special privilege to Scotland's equal status within the British Union. It builds on what was before. It is an addition to Scotland's Union status, not a subtraction!

The Union has only ever *added* to Scotland and its opportunities.

Next page: The Scots Guards at the Opening of the Scottish Parliament on 2-10-21.

PART 3

THE MANDATE MATTER

CHAPTER 7

WESTMINSTER'S UNITY MANDATES

The British Parliament, and the Government it forms, have mandates to keep the United Kingdom together, and a right, responsibility and duty to do so, and they shouldn't be shy to shout about it!

A "mandate" means "an authority to carry out a policy".

The SNP claims it has a "mandate" for a second referendum. The response from the British Government so far is that we've already had it, and "it was once in a generation, so let's move on."

The problem here is that saying "once in a generation" or "now is not the time", might knock things down the road, but it doesn't get to the nub of the matter.

Time will pass and a generation will come and go, and what should be said then?

Our advice to politicians is to avoid rhetoric which make it sound that a referendum "every generation" is some kind of accepted parliamentary convention. It suggests that the integrity of the United Kingdom should be regularly called into question. It suggests that attempts to break up the country should be regularly appeased.

The fact is, "once in a generation" or not, we don't want the existence of our One Big Country to be called into question in the first place.

"Now is not the time" because *never* is the time!

A better response is to point out that Westminster has several mandates to keep the UK together, and a right, responsibility and duty to do so, on behalf of everyone in the UK.

HERE'S 3 UNITY MANDATES

Pro-UK politicians should not be threatened by the nonsense that the Westminster Parliament has "no mandate" in Scotland, or has no right to try to hold the UK together.

Indeed, to say that the Union Parliament at Westminster, and the Government duly formed, does not have a mandate to govern any part of the UK is constitutionally and democratically illiterate.

It is also dangerous, because it suggests that our constitutionally and democratically-convened

Parliament, and the Government it forms, is somehow illegitimate.

Here's the truth.

The British Parliament has constitutional, democratic and popular mandates in Scotland, to govern Scotland, and to hold the UK together. It has a right, responsibility and duty to avoid endangering the future of the UK with another referendum.

Let's examine each in turn.

Constitutional Mandate: This means "relating to an established set of principles governing a state".

The established principle here is that every single person in Scotland who votes at a General Election for a candidate to go to Westminster, take the Oath, and sit in the Chamber – gives direct authority to that person to go there and govern for **all** the UK.

By voting to send someone to Westminster – whether that person is elected and whether that person is for or against Westminster – by doing that you are explicitly giving direct authority to the entire Parliament, which is eventually formed, to govern for all of the United Kingdom on your behalf.

That is the constitutional principle which holds the UK together. It is the constitutional principle which holds all democratic states together.

Democratic Mandate: The majority of people who vote at the British General Elections in Scotland do so for parties which want the UK to stay together. The SNP may get a majority of the MPs, but that's just the way the first-past-the-post system works.

Popular Mandate: A greater proportion of the electorate in Scotland vote at British General Elections than vote at Holyrood elections.

As we see from the graphic, this is always the case!

Westminster enjoys greater democratic legitimacy in Scotland, as measured by percentage turnout, than Holyrood!

Westminster General Election Turnout (Scotland)	Holyrood Election Turnout
2001 - 58.2%	1999 - 58.1%
2005 - 60.6%	2003 - 49.5%
2010 - 63.8%	2007 - 51.4%
2015 - 71.1%	2011 - 50.4%
2017 - 66.4%	2016 - 55.7%
2019 - 68.1%	2021 - 63.5%
Average = 64.7%	Average = 54.8%

Scottish Nationalists don't like to be reminded that we self-determine at the ballot box more with Westminster than with Holyrood.

Figures: wikipedia.org/wiki/Elections_in_Scotland   aForceForGood.UK

So there is no question that our collective Union Parliament has constitutional, democratic and popular mandates – given to it by the electorate of Scotland – to govern for all of the United Kingdom.

WESTMINSTER'S RIGHT, RESPONSIBILITY and DUTY on BEHALF OF US ALL

The potential break-up of Britain is a matter for us all, wherever we live in the UK (see chapter 4). We rely upon our collective Union Parliament at Westminster to make that understood.

It has a perfect right, responsibility and duty to hold the UK together on behalf of everyone who believes in the UK – and that's millions throughout our Islands, not just those in Scotland! It has a perfect right to say No to separation and Yes to a united Britain.

It is entirely proper for Parliament – and the Prime Minister and Government – to stand for the integrity, stability and security of the UK. Everyone in the United Kingdom who believes in the United Kingdom is **depending upon it** to do so!

That's its job. There is no other institution which can do this.

It is entirely constitutional and democratic for Westminster to avoid endangering the future of the UK with another referendum.

A WORD ABOUT the SENEDD

As per the graphic above, in 3 of the 6 elections since 1999, Holyrood failed to get over 52% of the electorate to vote for it!

In that regard, the Welsh Senedd, which spends billions of pounds of British Taxpayers money each year (almost £23bn in 23/24) has even less democratic legitimacy than Holyrood.

As the graphic below demonstrates, the Senedd has never managed to convince over half the Welsh electorate to even vote at its elections.

Even worse, it's never managed to convince even 47% of the Welsh electorate to vote for it!

The survival of the Senedd – a body which has very little democratic or popular legitimacy by any normal measure – is testament only to the British Parliament's desire to keep the devolution band-wagon rolling, regardless.

Westminster enjoys greater democratic legitimacy in Wales, as measured by percentage turnout, than the Senedd!

Westminster General Election Turnout (Wales)	Welsh Assembly/Senedd Election Turnout
2001 - 61.6%	1999 - 46.0%
2005 - 62.4%	2003 - 38.2%
2010 - 64.9%	2007 - 43.7%
2015 - 65.7%	2011 - 42.2%
2017 - 68.6%	2016 - 45.3%
2019 - 66.6%	2021 - 46.5%
Average = 65%	Average = 43.7%

The Senedd has never had a turnout of 47% of the electorate, let alone half!
The Welsh self-determine more with Westminster than with the Senedd.

Figures: wikipedia.org/wiki/Elections_in_Wales aForceForGood.UK

CHAPTER 8

BREAKING UP SHOULD BE HARD TO DO

Scottish nationalists are obsessed with breaking up the UK because the bar has been set so low. Here's how to change that.

Scottish nationalists believe that a one-off referendum, on one day, won by a simple numerical majority *is all that is required* for their ambition of an independent Scotland to be fulfilled.

The referendum on 18 September 2014 set the precedent!

It seems such an easy way to achieve their wildest dreams that it consumes them with its appeal – and we all suffer as a consequence.

Think about it!

The bar to the destruction of the centuries-young United Kingdom has been set extremely low. One referendum? Is that all it takes?

One referendum, regardless of turnout, and regardless of the majority – which could be anything from 1 person to a few hundred, can break-up the United Kingdom? (By the way, we don't hold to the idea that there would be any sort of "United Kingdom" left if Scotland broke away. The Scotland/England Union is the keystone of the United Kingdom.)

Is it really to be the case that the "ties that bind the UK together" are reduced to one flimsy thread of a referendum? It seems crazy when you think about it.

Naturally, seeing that the bar has been set so low, and seeing how easy it could be to achieve, the SNP and the Greens are **obsessed** with having another one, and if necessary another one, and so on, until they get their way.

Their obsession corrupts the entire Scottish body politic and shows no sign of going away.

By making it so easy for them, we are *encouraging* their obsession!

WHAT TO DO

To defeat obsession, you have to deny the reward. You have to put it out of reach. It seems painful at first, but eventually it works.

If we want their referendum obsession to go away, then **we must put their reward out of reach.** It must be extremely difficult for them to achieve their prize.

First, this means a second referendum should be avoided. This means it must be extremely difficult, legally and democratically, to achieve one.

Second, if it is allowed, then there has to be a variety of additional road blocks to overcome which prevent an easy break-up; that is, constitutional hurdles which stand in the way of separation, such as required thresholds on turnout and majority.

Third, even if such a referendum were to be won by the separatists, then it should not be the end of the matter. It should require a follow-up General Election where the people advocating separation must win a majority of the seats and a majority of the votes on an abstentionist platform – that is, where they refuse to take up their seats if elected.

The point is that breaking up the UK has to involve more than being granted a referendum on the basis of a questionable "mandate", and then winning a one-off referendum, on one day, with a simple numerical majority, which could represent a tiny number of people in Scotland, and a miniscule proportion of the overall UK electorate!

So we need our politicians to state the following regularly: **We do not believe, nor do we accept, that the UK can be broken up by a one-off referendum, on one day, won by a simple numerical majority!**

HAVE A STRONG 'PHILOSOPHY OF UNION'

Let our politicians stand up and say that the United Kingdom is a Unitary State and One Nation which cannot and should not be defeated by a simple one-off political device, such as a referendum.

Let them declare that it is a far more unitary, stable and permanent creation than hitherto some have imagined, or try to pretend.

Let's not fall for the notion that the UK is merely some kind of "temporary arrangement" which can, and should, be constantly open to debate.

For example, many Scottish nationalists are always saying that the UK is "not a nation, but a political state".

This makes it easier for them to advocate the unravelling of this political state.

They take the view that it is some kind of "provisional" structure – existing only at the present moment – where we agree to get along *for the time being*; and that it is "conditional" – that it exists only upon certain requirements which must always be met.

Imagine if the United States of America – which could be argued to be 50 little countries – took that view. Imagine if the USA were to allow their States to secede by simply having a vote in a one-off referendum. There could be States seceding all the time. The USA would be thrown into absolute chaos.

Instead, the USA makes it extremely difficult, if not impossible, for a State to secede legally. The USA is not a "provisional" and "conditional" relationship and consequently holds together fairly well. Nobody is seriously worried about any State breaking away – at least not any time soon.

Indeed, no country can survive for long on an assumption that its existence is merely "provisional", as if it is "only a matter of time", or "conditional" upon favourable circumstances at a certain moment.

Thankfully, authentic Unionists such as **A Force For Good** believe the UK to be **One Big Country and a Nation.**

We believe the UK represents something **substantial and integral** beyond a mere "political state"; something that can't simply be pulled apart; something that is joined together by many ties that bind; social, cultural, historic, economic, constitutional; something that can't be defeated merely by a one-off referendum, on one day, won by a simple numerical majority!

Our frame is far more solid. It is harder to break.

We see the United Kingdom as **a Nation of Unions** not just a "Union of Nations".

We see the United Kingdom as **a Nation of Families** not just a "Family of Nations".

In this regard, it doesn't matter which view is "absolutely correct" – our view or the Scottish nationalist view. The fact is that there is no cosmic arbiter on this particular question. All that matters is which view *you* hold to, work from, and promote in physical reality.

We encourage our politicians to have a properly-formed **unitary understanding** of the UK which *works naturally* to hold us together; to see the UK as a genuine Nation in and of itself, which has **a right to be properly protected against the referendum device by a range of legal, democratic and constitutional safeguards.**

It's our job at A Force For Good to help develop and articulate these legal, democratic and constitutional "locks" which help to safeguard our "Union Settlement".

OPPONENTS of the UK UNDERSTAND the WEAKNESS

As usual, the people who understand most clearly this weakness in elements of the British political class, are those who are most opposed to our One Big Country. For example, Gerry Adams was unfortunately correct when he noted:

> "It's now quite clear that the so-called United Kingdom is held together by a thread. And that thread can be unravelled as a result of referenda in Scotland, or elsewhere or indeed in Ireland." (1)

Well, that's not good enough! We can't have a Nation which is held together so precariously, and which can be destroyed so easily by a one-off referendum, on one day, won by a simple numerical majority.

WORKED EXAMPLE: HOW a TINY NUMBER of PEOPLE COULD BREAK-UP the UK

Consider how few people could be involved in ending the UK at another referendum. Let's crunch the numbers!

Here are the latest electoral figures available (Dec 2022) at the ONS website. (2) We are using the "Local government electoral registrations" figures.

Overall UK Electorate: 48,820,571
Electorate in Scotland: 4,243,803

We've chosen the local government figures, since the 2014 referendum was run on this franchise. Let us presume the same turnout as in 2014, which was 85% rounded up. This means that 3,607,233 people would vote in Scotland.

Say a second referendum was won by the Scottish nationalists by 51-49 per cent, although it could be even closer. This means there would be 51% of 3,607,233 = **1,839,689** people in Scotland voting to break-up the UK.

This winning number would represent a minuscule 3.77% of the overall UK electorate!

Even if the winning figures from 2014 were reversed and 55% voted to break-up, that would still only be 1,983,979 (which is also *a minority* of the overall Scottish electorate) and 4.06% of the overall UK electorate.

In what democratic universe does it make sense for 3.77% – say 4% – of a nation's electorate to break-up the entire country? It would be morally wrong.

IN CONCLUSION

The UK is more than a voluntary Union bound by consent. It is also – by necessity – a legal Union bound by laws. We must be bound by law because we're all involved, wherever we live in our One Big Country. We all have a stake and that stake must be considered and protected by law.

And thank goodness, because pro-UK folk need to know that we're held together by something more substantial than the momentary whim of a minority of the Scottish electorate, at a one-off referendum, on one day, which could be won by a tiny margin, with a total of around 4%, or less, of the entire UK electorate.

The British Parliament has a perfect right, responsibility and duty to assert law in order to avoid such a potential democratic farce, and to keep us all together, and it has several mandates to do so, as we point out in chapter 7.

Right now, because the referendum route to "indy" seems so tantalisingly easy, the SNP and their supporters obsess about it. Their obsession consumes them, to the detriment of the rest of Scottish society.

If the route to destroying the UK was much harder, then a lot of them would lose their enthusiasm; a lot of the puff, obsession and fundamentalism would go out of their movement.

As they naturally deflate, many of them would relax and concentrate on having a normal life.

At that stage, we could approach something resembling a normal country again!

1. BBC Radio Ulster 'Inside Politics' programme, reported by Stephen Walker, BBC NI political reporter, "Gerry Adams: United Kingdom union hanging by a thread", 7-2-14. See video from 0.52 at bbc.co.uk/news/uk-northern-ireland-26082515

2. Office of National Statistics, "Electoral statistics for the UK", Table 1 in the Excel spreadsheet at tinyurl.com/mrx269e5

CHAPTER 9

THE SNP AND ITS "MANDATES"

How real are they? We examine the 8 elections since 2007, and show that the SNP has never had over 36% of the entire electorate at any election!

The SNP is always telling us that it has a "mandate" for a second referendum based upon the number of people who vote for it at elections. A "mandate" means "an authority to carry out a policy".

A proper mandate to hold a referendum for something as serious as trying to break up the United Kingdom would have to include, *at least*, 50% of **the entire electorate** (not just the turnout) plus 1.

In this chapter, we examine the SNP results in 8 elections in Scotland since 2007 – the year in which it took power. These were the Holyrood Elections in 2007, 2011, 2016, and 2021 and the General Elections in 2010, 2015, 2017 and 2019.

We're excluding the 2014 referendum on separation and the 2016 referendum on Brexit. (1)

We're going to examine **the percentage of the entire electorate** who voted specifically for the SNP at these elections, and we'll see if it comes anywhere close to 50%+1 of the entire voting public. We'll also note the SNP voters on the day, expressed as **a percentage of the actual turnout**.

In this way, we'll have some idea of the exact "mandate" which the SNP is attempting to claim.

The FRANCHISE

The size of the entire electorate for Holyrood is different than Westminster. EU citizens are allowed to vote at Holyrood elections; and since the May 2016 election inclusive, 16-year-olds in Scotland have been able to vote at Holyrood elections but not at Westminster elections.

HOLYROOD ELECTIONS

How they work: Each person has two votes: one for the local Constituency (of which there are 73, decided by first-past-the-post) and one for the Region in which he or she resides, of which there are 8 throughout Scotland (electing 56 MSPs, decided by proportional representation).

In all cases since 2007 inclusive, the vote for the SNP is lower on the Regional Ballot than the vote for the SNP in the Constituency ballot. This suggests that some SNP voters use their second vote for another party which might be sympathetic to separation. This is likely to work the other way too, with some people voting for, say, the Greens in their Constituency and for the SNP in their Region.

Since each person has two votes, we need to **take an average of the Constituency and Regional vote for the SNP** to obtain an average figure for the number of people who "vote SNP".

Holyrood Electorate Figures: We are using the voting, electorate and turnout figures listed in the tables for each year, beginning in 2007 at wikipedia.org/wiki/2007_Scottish_Parliament_electi on

You can find each subsequent election by replacing the year in the URL with the year of election. (2) The turnout figures include the spoilt votes (which in 2007, for example, were high).

HOLYROOD 3 May 2007
To find the total SNP Vote expressed as a % of **the Electorate**:
Total SNP Constituency vote: 664,227
Total SNP Regional vote: 633,611
Average SNP vote = 648,919
Electorate: 3,899,472

SNP vote as % of Electorate = 16.6% (Average SNP vote of 648,919 divided by Electorate x 100.)

To find the total SNP Vote expressed as a % of **the Turnout**:
Constituencies: 2,102,609 (all voters)
Regions: 2,104,842 (all voters)
Average Turnout = 2,103,726

SNP vote as % of Turnout = 30.8%. (Average SNP vote of 648,919 divided by Average Turnout x 100.)

That is, in 2007, the SNP took power on less than a third of the voters on the day, which was less than 17% of the entire electorate!
    It is astonishing to think that less than 17% of the entire electorate is responsible for setting Scotland along the lines we have endured.

HOLYROOD 5 May 2011
Total SNP Constituency vote: 902,915
Total SNP Regional vote: 876,421
Average SNP vote = 889,668
Electorate: 3,950,626
SNP vote as % of Electorate = 22.5%

Constituencies: 1,995,639
Regions: 1,996,823
Average Turnout = 1,996,231
SNP vote as % of Turnout = 44.6%

HOLYROOD 5 May 2016

Total SNP Constituency vote: 1,059,898
Total SNP Regional vote: 953,587
Average SNP vote = 1,006,743
Electorate: 4,099,907. This was the first Holyrood
election when 16-year-olds were allowed to vote.
SNP vote as % of Electorate = 24.6%

Constituencies: 2,288,369
Regions: 2,289,564
Average Turnout = 2,288,967
SNP vote as % of Turnout = 44%

This was a year after its Westminster election
victory – when the SNP was riding high –
rejuvenated and fresh from its failure at the 2014
referendum. Yet it still failed to gain the support of
even a quarter of the electorate in Scotland.

HOLYROOD 6 May 2021

Total SNP Constituency vote: 1,291,204
Total SNP Regional vote: 1,094,374
Average SNP vote = 1,192,789
Electorate: 4,280,785
SNP vote as % of Electorate = 27.9%

Constituencies: 2,716,785
Regions: 2,718,065
Average Turnout = 2,717,425
SNP vote as % of Turnout = 43.9%

During these 4 elections we can note that the average SNP vote was rising. Since 2011 it had been around 44% of the Turnout.

However, when measured against the entire electorate, it is low, and never reached 28%, or even 30%, let alone one third, of all the potential voters in Scotland.

That is, the SNP has never had 1 in 3 people, or even 3 in 10 people, voting for it at Holyrood elections.

Now let's turn our attention to the 4 Westminster General Elections in this period.

WESTMINSTER ELECTIONS

There were 59 seats in Scotland by first-past-the-post. This changed in 2024 to 57.

The SNP voting figures, and the overall turnout figures are from wikipedia.org/wiki/Elections_in_Scotland (3)

The sources for the electorate each year are referenced below.

WESTMINSTER 6 May 2010

SNP Vote: 491,386
Electorate (4): 3,863,042
Turnout: 2,465,722
SNP vote as % of Electorate = 12.7%
SNP vote as % of Turnout = 19.9%

WESTMINSTER 7 May 2015
SNP Vote: 1,454,436
Electorate (5): 4,099,532
Turnout: 2,910,465
SNP vote as % of Electorate = 35.5%
SNP vote as % of Turnout = 49.97%

This was the high-water-mark of the SNP's success and its vote represented 35.5% of the total Westminster Parliament electorate in Scotland at the time – a little over a third.

WESTMINSTER 8 June 2017
SNP Vote: 977,569
Electorate (6): 3,988,441
Turnout: 2,649,695
SNP vote as % of Electorate = 24.5%
SNP vote as % of Turnout = 36.9%

The SNP total vote dropped by an astonishing 476,867 from the 2015 election!

WESTMINSTER 12 December 2019
SNP Vote: 1,242,380
Electorate (7): 4,053,056
Turnout: 2,759,061
SNP vote as % of Electorate = 30.7%
SNP vote as % of Turnout = 45%

KEY TAKEAWAYS

a. The SNP has never had more than 28% of the electorate at Holyrood elections. It has never had more than 1 in 3 people vote for it at Holyrood elections.

b. The SNP has never had more than 45% of the turnout at Holyrood elections.

c. The SNP vote at Westminster grew considerably between the years 2010-2015 as a result of being granted a referendum and enjoying the political dynamic which came from that opportunity; and in the aftermath, the chance to argue and complain over the extent of "new powers" granted to it (unnecessarily) by the British Parliament, thereby ensuring it continued to hold the initiative and dominate the debate.

d. The SNP has never had more than 36% of the electorate vote for it at Westminster elections.

e. Although it came close in 2015, the SNP has never had over 50% of the turnout at Westminster elections.

f. Before we accept that the SNP has a "mandate" for another referendum to try to break up the United Kingdom, we should insist on, at least, 50% plus 1 of *the entire electorate* before we would even *consider* such a momentous decision.

g. As we argue in the next chapter, this should only apply if the party attains this vote, at a British General Election, with a majority of MPs, who are all standing on an Abstentionist platform!

1. At the UK Membership Referendum on Thursday 18 September 2014: The 'Yes' to breaking up the UK vote was 1,617,989 (44.7%) and the 'No' to breaking up the UK vote was 2,001,926 (55.3%), with 3,429 spoiled. The electorate numbered 4,283,392, which included 16-year-olds for the first time. The turnout was 84.6%, the highest recorded turnout for an election or referendum in the UK since universal suffrage.

At the UK Independence Referendum on 23 June 2016, the 'Remain" in the EU vote was 1,661,191 (62%) and the 'Leave' the EU vote was 1,018,322 (38%), with 1,666 spoiled. That is, despite the entire political and media establishment in Scotland being pro-Remain, over 1 million people still voted for UK Independence. The electorate numbered 3,987,112, which did *not* include 16-year-olds or EU citizens. The turnout was 67.25%.

2. We are using the figures from this series of pages since the Scottish elections page at wikipedia.org/wiki/Elections_in_Scotland appears to be in error for the year 2007, since it lists the same electorate for both 2007 and 2011.

3. These figures do not include the spoilt votes, but neither do those on the series of pages starting at wikipedia.org/wiki/2005_United_Kingdom_general_election_in_Scotland

4. electionresults.parliament.uk/election/2010-05-06/results/Location/Country/Scotland

5. electionresults.parliament.uk/election/2015-05-07/results/Location/Country/Scotland

6. electionresults.parliament.uk/election/2017-06-08/results/Location/Country/Scotland

7. electionresults.parliament.uk/election/2019-12-12/results/Location/Country/Scotland

HOLYROOD

3 May 2007

SNP vote as % of Electorate = **16.6%**

SNP vote as % of Turnout = **30.8%**

5 May 2011

SNP vote as % of Electorate = **22.5%**

SNP vote as % of Turnout = **44.6%**

5 May 2016

SNP vote as % of Electorate = **24.6%**

SNP vote as % of Turnout = **44%**

6 May 2021

SNP vote as % of Electorate = **27.9%**

SNP vote as % of Turnout = **43.9%**

WESTMINSTER

6 May 2010

SNP vote as % of Electorate = **12.7%**

SNP vote as % of Turnout = **19.9%**

7 May 2015

SNP vote as % of Electorate = **35.5%**

SNP vote as % of Turnout = **49.97%**

8 June 2017

SNP vote as % of Electorate = **24.5%**

SNP vote as % of Turnout = **36.9%**

12 December 2019

SNP vote as % of Electorate = **30.7%**

SNP vote as % of Turnout = **45%**

CHAPTER 10

DEBUNKING THE SNP "MANDATES"

Here are all the ways in which the SNP try to claim a mandate to "open negotiations" for a second referendum; all the ways they try to claim the "authority to carry out their policy". As we have shown in chapter 7, the British Union Parliament also has mandates to keep the UK together and to refuse such a dangerous policy.

1. Declare that "the Scottish people are sovereign and so they have a right to self-determination"
That's not a sufficient mandate, since the electorate in Scotland regularly exercises its powers of self-determination to *maintain* the Union!

After all, if we understand "sovereign" to mean "having supreme power residing in itself", and "self-determination" to mean "the power of a population to decide its own government and political relations or of an individual to live his own life" (*Chambers 20th Century*), then, as we've seen in chapter 7 the electorate in Scotland has consistently used its democratic sovereignty and self-determination to vote for parties and people who want to keep the UK together.

Long may that continue!

"MANDATES" at WESTMINSTER

2. Ensure the SNP has an outright Majority of Scottish MPs at a General Election. This requires at least 29 SNP MPs to form the majority of 57.

At its Conference in Aberdeen on 15 October 2023, the SNP voted to adopt this strategy for 2024. It also agreed that the words "Independence for Scotland" would appear next to the SNP's name and logo on the ballot paper, thereby boosting the claim that everyone will know what they are voting for.

3. Ensure the SNP has the Most Scottish MPs at a General Election

There are 57 MPs elected to Westminster from Scotland. Having the most MPs means, for example, 22 SNP, 20 Labour, 10 Conservative, 5 Lib Dems. This would be an even weaker mandate than above.

4. SNP gets the Majority of the Vote on the Day at a General Election

This was Nicola Sturgeon's "de facto referendum". The SNP would campaign on the single proposal that Scotland should be "independent". A mandate would be claimed if the SNP achieved more than 50% of the vote on the day (regardless of turnout). As we have seen in chapter 9, they came close to this at the General Election in 2015, although it was nowhere near a majority of the overall electorate.

5. Abstain! Do what Sinn Fein did at the British General Election of 14 December 1918

Of the 105 Westminster seats in Ireland, Sinn Fein won 73, with the Home Rule Party winning 6, and Unionists taking 26. Sinn Fein refused to take up their seats, and its MPs (those who were not in prison) convened the First Dail in Dublin on 21 January 1919.

This option appeals to the Irish republican element of Scottish nationalism, even though there are significant differences between Scotland today and Ireland in 1918!

A democratic difference is that Sinn Fein stood on an explicitly abstentionist policy. Its manifesto prior to the election of 1918 stated that the aim was to establish a Republic by "withdrawing the Irish Representation from the British Parliament" and establish "a constituent assembly comprising persons chosen by Irish constituencies as the supreme national authority to speak and act in the name of the Irish people". (1)

If the SNP want to follow this path, then it would have to become an abstentionist party.

6. "Get elected and then Walk Out"

It would be entirely wrong for SNP MPs to be elected on the assumption that they will take up their seats at Westminster on behalf of their constituents, and then, once elected with a mandate to sit in the Parliament, decide not to sit, or walk out in a huff, half way through.

This would only be legitimate democratic behaviour if they made clear their abstentionist policy prior to being elected.

"MANDATES" at HOLYROOD
7. Assert that "Holyrood democracy trumps Westminster Democracy"

Some argue that the democratic authority of Holyrood somehow trumps Westminster on matters relating to Scotland. They claim this because Holyrood is specifically focused on matters relating to Scotland. To argue this point, you'd have to:
a) Ignore the constitutional fact that Holyrood is a devolved arm of the British Parliament (chapter 6).
b) Argue that Scotland exists in a vacuum and has nothing to do with the rest of the UK; that it somehow has no constitutional, democratic, or moral connection or involvement with the rest of

the UK, and that the rest of the UK has no connections with Scotland; connections and involvement which are literally made manifest in the Union Parliament itself.

c) Deny the constitutional, democratic and popular "Unity Mandates" which Westminster enjoys in Scotland, which we outlined in chapter 7.

8. Ensure the Separation Side has an outright Majority of MSPs at Holyrood

There are 129 MSPs. This would require at least 65 MSPs in an SNP/Green coalition.

9. Ensure the Separation Side has the Most MSPs at Holyrood

Having the most MSPs means, say, SNP 50, Labour 40, Conservative 25, Lib Dem 10 and Green 4. This would be an even weaker "mandate" than above.

10. Ensure the Separation Side gets a Majority of the Vote on the Day at a Holyrood Election

The next Holyrood election is scheduled for May 2026. It is possible that the SNP and Greens will treat this as a "de facto referendum", and a mandate would be claimed if together they achieved more than 50% of the vote on the day (regardless of turnout).

As we've seen in chapter 9 they haven't come close to this at Holyrood elections, and turnouts are always very low. Therefore, even if they achieved such a feat, it would still be *a minority* of the overall electorate. In 2021, less than a third of the overall electorate in Scotland put the SNP/Green coalition in power. (2)

11. Two-Thirds of Holyrood MSPs to vote for a Holyrood Election and hold it on this one Topic

If a very large number of SNP/Green MSPs were particularly annoyed that they were not being granted a second referendum, then, according to "Section 3.1 Extraordinary general elections" of the Scotland Act 1998, a two-thirds majority (86 MSPs) could vote for an immediate Holyrood election, and then campaign specifically upon the matter of a second referendum.

12. First Minister to Resign and force a Holyrood Election on this one Topic

According to the same section of the Scotland Act, if the First Minister resigns, then Holyrood has to elect a new FM within 28 days.

If a majority SNP/Green coalition voted down any replacement offered by the opposition, then a Holyrood election would have to follow.

Both of these latter options are somewhat chaotic and unlikely, and not certain to deliver the result intended.

For example, when Edward Heath called a snap General Election in 1974, he lost.

When Teresa May tried to capitalise on Labour's problems in 2017, she lost her overall majority.

Now we get to the even crazier options.

OTHER "MANDATE" NOTIONS
13. "Unilateral Declaration of Independence": Just hold a Referendum anyway, even if it's Unlawful
Only problems for the SNP are that:
a) The returning officers in the local authorities – many of which are not SNP-controlled – would not obey an illegal instruction.
b) Most pro-UK folk would boycott it, and
c) it would not be recognised by the international community.

14. Appeal to International Law on the basis that Scotland has a "Right to Self-Determination"
The SNP took this claim to the Supreme Court. Its judgement on 23 November 2023 found that a referendum on the Union was a matter reserved to the UK Parliament. It also found that the International Law which upholds the concept of self-determination is not relevant, and does not apply to Scotland's situation.

Scotland and its people are not colonial subjects, or oppressed, or denied access to modern democratic expression, or treated unequally, or discriminated against – despite what some Scottish nationalists like to fantasise.

And as we say again, most Scots exercise their right to self-determination by determining to stay in the Union anyway!

15. Hold a Referendum if Opinion Polls consistently show over 60% support for one

This is politically ridiculous. Opinion polls are not democratic. They have no safeguards. They create opinion as much as reflect it; they ensure the subject matter and the questions can be easily biased; they are the playthings of wealthy political interests; and they are highlighted by media outlets which have their own biases to promote. Yet this absurd "route to a mandate" has been seriously suggested by some unionists and nationalists.

AND FINALLY, THE BIGGEST DANGER

16. A UK Government will Create a Route when it Suits its Purposes

A Labour Government, desperate for the support of the SNP to carry through its agenda (see chapter 14) might well do a deal to offer a referendum. Or it could continue devolving powers to Holyrood to the point where it deliberately, or thoughtlessly, devolves the legal power to hold a referendum without the permission of the Union Parliament.

That's why we must never rest!

THE UNION PARLIAMENT IS THE PLACE!

Holyrood is not the proper place to seek a mandate for a second referendum. The British Union Parliament is the proper place to seek a mandate which is constitutional, moral and democratic for all the people of the UK.

After all, "independence" is about MPs from Scotland being removed from the British Union Parliament. That's what "independence" would mean constitutionally. So the Union Parliament is the place to seek the mandate to remove them.

Secondly, Holyrood is a devolved Parliament. It is not equal and opposite to Westminster. It does not have the same powers as Westminster. Although Scottish nationalists don't like to be reminded of the fact, the political relationship is vertical not horizontal.

To get a mandate for a second referendum, the SNP would need to stand on no other issue than the issue of demanding a second referendum; and it would have to do so at a British General Election; and it would have to do so on an abstentionist policy; and it would only acquire a mandate if it won a majority of the seats with a majority of the electorate.

Then, and only then, could we start to think about having another referendum. And even if we had one, and even if they managed to overcome all the necessary hurdles, and even if they won it, then there would still need to be an immediate General

Election, and the SNP would need to stand again on the same abstentionist platform, in order to confirm that this is indeed what the people want, and they'd have to win that one again with a majority of the seats and a majority of the electorate.

You see, we're not making it easy for them! **For our part, we must keep promoting the value and benefits of our wonderful United Kingdom in order to drive up our support from 55% to 65% and more, in order that we render the question of another referendum irrelevant in the first place!**

1. Issued by the Standing Committee of Sinn Fein, "General Election. Manifesto to the Irish People", at Trinity College Dublin, at tinyurl.com/y5xe3rn4

2. Truth about the 2nd Ref "Mandate", 20-11-22, at aforceforgood.uk/single-post/truth-about-mandate

Next page: Our colourful Street Stalls help to boost pro-UK morale in the heart of the Great British City of Glasgow, 20-8-22.

PART 4

RULES FOR PRO-UK POLITICIANS

CHAPTER 11

DON'T SPEAK SEPARATION INTO EXISTENCE

Pro-UK politicians must learn to use "Union Frames" in their rhetoric – frames which encourage us to think of unity. They must not use the Scottish nationalist, or federalist frames, which encourage us to think of separation. Statements, ideas and policies must be articulated in a manner which helps the UK to stay together. Otherwise they risk speaking separation into existence.

Prior to the SNP winning the 3 May 2007 Holyrood Election, the collective term for the people who run Holyrood was "the Scottish Executive". "Executive" is a word which refers to those who have the power to put decisions and laws into effect.

They were not termed a "government". This was to avoid confusion with the actual Government of the United Kingdom.

The aim was to emphasise that there was a difference in political power between the administration in Holyrood and the central Union Parliament in London.

On Monday 3 September 2007, four months after taking power, Alex Salmond changed the name of the Scottish Executive – officially at Holyrood, but not legally in law – to "Scottish Government".

He did this because he could!

Due to the upside-down "Devolution Settlement" – which we examined in chapter 5 – nobody had thought to write down that he couldn't!

As he has since said that there was nothing "legally" to stop him, and that it was "a small example of political will". (1)

This was a considerable change in language, and it caused people to think of the constitutional relationship in a new manner.

It caused a psychological move away from thinking of Holyrood as a devolved arm of the British Parliament (which it was, and which it remains) and towards a misapprehension that Holyrood was a separate and sovereign entity, in an equal and opposite position to Westminster.

This name change was subsequently approved by the Calman Commission (Dec 2007-

June 2009) which was composed of people who wanted to move the UK towards a more "federal" relationship. Unfortunately, their report persuaded David Cameron to write the name change into law in his Scotland Act 2012 (para. 12).

This has hugely compromised our understanding of the devolved relationship.

1. It changes political perception from the fact of a central British Parliament and Government with devolved arms, to the notion of the UK as already some kind of Federal State with different "Governments" all equal and opposite and competing with each other.

2. It creates an equivalency with the British Government which does not exist in real life – because the SNP and Green administration does not have the independent powers of a "Government".

3. It gives the misimpression that Westminster and Holyrood are in a horizontal and equal political power relationship with each other. This muddies the distinction between Holyrood as a devolved parliament or an equal parliament. It undermines and misrepresents the actual constitutional and devolved relationship (chapter 5).

4. It normalises the idea of the SNP and Green administration, as an equal and opposite

Government to the British Government which – and this is crucial – leads people to believe that it should have the same powers.

5. It normalises the idea of Holyrood as an entirely separate and sovereign Parliament which leads people to wonder why Scotland is not already independent.

6. This then sets up a conflict which gives the impression that this is about "the Scottish Parliament versus the British Parliament", or "Scotland versus the rest of the UK"; rather than what it should be about, which is the Scottish Parliament working amicably within the British Parliament's overall ambit, responsibility and guardianship for the betterment of everyone throughout our Islands.

7. This conflict sets up Holyrood as a "subjugated equivalent" and feeds the separatist narrative. The SNP trick has been to portray Scotland's relationship with the rest of the United Kingdom, since 1707, as a form of subjugation, as we examined in chapter 6. This is deliberately intended to encourage the attitudes that would normally accompany such an unfortunate situation.

The reality is that Scotland's position within the Union is one of generous added privileges – such as a powerful devolved Parliament.

But still the SNP try to pretend that the remainder of the reserved powers held at Westminster are equivalent to "oppression" and "subjugation". They are still able to make considerable capital on these reserved powers – and of course they always will, regardless of how few, or how many, remain.

8. Criticism of "the Scottish Government" can sound like "talking Scotland down". When an MP or MSP criticises "the Scottish Government", then bristles will rise. It risks a knee-jerk reaction among those who only hear the words "the Scottish". But the listener won't bother if you criticise "the SNP Government" or better still "the SNP administration" or even better, the politician by name. Indeed, chances are, they'll agree with you! See the difference?

9. Using the phrase "Scottish Government" is to ignore and abdicate the British Parliament's role as the actual and ultimate "Government of Scotland". This is so important to grasp! The British Parliament, and the Government it forms, *is* the ultimate government of Scotland. Therefore, every time a UK Government minister uses the phrase "Scottish Government" to refer only to Holyrood, then a little bit of the UK Government's ability to govern Scotland dies!

Every time politicians in Westminster speak about "the Scottish Government" as something different from themselves then they are abdicating the Parliament's position as the ultimate government of Scotland.

Perhaps most of them don't realise they are doing this because they don't properly understand devolution. Perhaps they don't realise that what they call "the Scottish Government" is simply a devolved arm of the British Parliament itself. Perhaps they don't properly understand the Constitution of the British Union, which we explained in chapter 5.

This continued misuse of words helps to empower the separatists. The least we can do now is to avoid falling into this trap.

DON'T SAY "the SCOTTISH GOVERNMENT" or "Our TWO GOVERNMENTS"

To pretend that we have two equal heads on one body is to corrupt the reality of our constitutional relationship.

Every time a pro-UK politician speaks about "Scotland's two governments" or "both our governments" then they only amplify the nationalist view of things.

They are speaking within a separatist and federalist frame, not a Union frame!

It is also to confound our ability to argue for

the Union. After all, if the SNP and Greens really have formed "a Government", then why is it not in control of an independent country? That's the conclusion the phrase is urging us towards!

If we are being led to believe that something called the Scottish "Government" is on the same plane of political power as the British Government, then of course we're going to wonder why the Scottish "Government" is not getting its way all the time.

It will lead us to believe that the only reason the Scottish "Government" does not have the powers of the apparently equivalent British Government, must be something to do with it being denied its rightful powers.

Such rhetoric just feeds the false narrative that "it's because we're being kept down" – that Holyrood is some sort of **subjugated equivalent**.

Hence the reason we have people who imagine that an SNP/Green majority at Holyrood is somehow a "mandate" to have a referendum to break up Britain.

Hence the reason we have people genuinely confused as to why Holyrood cannot hold a referendum to break up Britain without the agreement of the central British Parliament.

Over time, such deliberate constitutional mislabelling and misrepresentation has only succeeded in a confusion which feeds the separatist grievance machine.

A minor rhetorical change has had massive implications for the political debate.

WHAT SHOULD WE SAY INSTEAD?

We can use the term "devolved Scottish administration" or "the devolved SNP/Green coalition" or "devolved SNP/Green administration" or "Holyrood's devolved administration" or "the devolved Scottish Executive".

That puts the correct constitutional relationship into words again.

If you don't want to go the whole hog and start referring to the SNP and Greens as an "administration", or an "executive", then at least do what you can to emphasise the fact that they are a "*devolved* government".

At least do what you can to emphasise the correct constitutional relationship!

This is an essential part of the push-back against separatism. We have to start using terminology which does not mislabel, misrepresent and confuse the constitutional relationship.

Let's give you a for-instance.

A LESSON in HOW to DESCRIBE and LABEL PROPERLY

As far as the British Parliament is concerned, there has been no consistent effort to explain the correct relationship. Indeed, the British Government is as guilty as anyone in promoting the confusion.

We see it every day, and it needs to change!

Every time a pro-UK MP, or MSP, talks about "the Scottish Government" instead of even bothering to stress "the *devolved* Scottish Government" then they miss **a teaching moment** and they compound the problem.

Every time the Prime Minister criticises "the Scottish Government" for doing something wrong, then he misses an open goal to specifically draw attention to his political opponents **by personal name and party affiliation.**

For example, in an article in the *Daily Telegraph*, the PM Rishi Sunak was quoted as saying:

> "What we do now know is that **the Scottish Government** does not want to support the Scottish energy industry and the 200,000 jobs that it produces." (2)

His point was correct, but he absolutely misses the target which is his political rivals, the SNP/Green coalition, who also have personal, and party, names! When presented with an open goal, he hits the post and the ball rebounds into his face. So let's rephrase it for him:

"What we do now know is that **the devolved SNP and Green coalition led by Nicola Sturgeon and Patrick Harvie** do not want to support the Scottish energy industry and the 200,000 jobs that it produces."

Hear how much better that sounds! Hear how much more meaningful that sounds. Hear how much more accurate and incisive that sounds!

It describes the proper devolved relationship while naming the guilty parties and persons! Not only is it teaching about our constitution, it is also hitting home politically against his opponents by name, while at the same time avoiding the confusing and misleading phrase "Scottish Government".

AVOID FEDERALIST FRAMING such as "SHARED GOVERNMENT"

"Shared government" is a phrase used throughout Gordon Brown's plans for the Labour Party, examined in chapter 14.

This is a federalist frame. It is encouraging separate "governments" for all parts of the UK.

It is not a unitary frame. It does not mean unitary government – which is to say, government of a Unitary State; "a sovereign state governed as a single entity in which the central government is the supreme authority." (Wikipedia)

For example, when we were in the EU we had a "shared government" with 27 other nations, but we were not in a unitary state, with a unitary parliament and government, as in the UK.

So let's not allow this federalist phrase to be flown in under the radar!

IN SUMMARY – STEP UP TO THE MIC!
Politicians, you've got the microphone.

Every time you rise to speak, use it as a teaching moment; an opportunity to articulate the correct constitutional relationship and to strengthen it for the good of our One Big Country.

Use a Union Frame, not a Separatist Frame. Speak unity, not separation, into existence!

1. See Alex Salmond explain at "Scottish Government versus Scottish Executive", on our youtube.com/watch?v=Y5Rnj9xbwaw The video is from a meeting circa 5 October 2022.

2. Simon Johnson "PM accuses Sturgeon of abandoning the North Sea", *The Daily Telegraph*, (Scottish edition), 12-1-23.

Next Page: A Force For Good has become adept at using the most effective rhetoric as a result of speaking with the Great British Public at our regular

Street Stalls. Pictured are some of our friendly and fashionable AFFG Legends in Glasgow, 18-6-22.

Our T-shirts and Hoodies are available via the link at aforceforgood.uk/shop-1

CHAPTER 12

THREE EASY-WIN POLICIES FOR THE UNION

We've put together 3 urgent and easy-win policies to help the Government strengthen the Union of the UK, and one bonus policy. There's no excuse not to be doing all of these things, and more!

The aim is to strengthen the ties that bind our One Big Country together politically, economically, socially and culturally, and to defeat the separatists.

1. DITCH THE NORTHERN IRELAND PROTOCOL

The SNP/Greens and Sinn Fein want to re-join the EU. In order to keep the UK together, we must ensure that it becomes as hard as possible for these parties to advocate this policy.

That means we must ensure that there is the maximum integration of trade and travel and social and cultural matters, between *all parts* of the UK.

So long as Northern Ireland remains under EU authority, then it means that when the rest of the UK moves away from the EU, then Northern Ireland will move away from the rest of the UK!

This will make it harder for Northern Ireland to "re-join" the rest of the UK, and easier for Sinn Fein to promote integration with the EU, and integration with the Republic of Ireland.

If we are to keep the UK together, then Northern Ireland must move in the same direction, and at the same pace, as the rest of the UK.

Similarly, in Scotland: As the UK moves away from the EU, then it makes it much harder for the SNP and Greens to argue to re-join the EU, since the upheaval of re-joining would be so much greater.

However, if the UK does not substantially diverge from the EU, then it will make it easier for the separatists to advocate re-joining because "nothing much would be changing".

2. BRAND UK PAYMENTS BRITISH – which means OVERHAUL HMRC'S BLAND COMMUNICATIONS

The positive power of the British Treasury to create money and to get it to people in Scotland is not being properly explained and promoted.

The British Government must stop getting the easy things wrong!

Case in point: During the Covid period, the Furlough, and Self-Employment Income Support Schemes missed an opportunity to promote Britishness and the value and benefits of the United Kingdom.

During 2020 and 2021 there were large numbers of people in Scotland claiming furlough, and self-employment support, from Her Majesty's Revenue and Customs, via its webpages.

According to a report in *The Scotsman* (11-6-20) Treasury figures revealed that around 628,000 furloughed Scottish workers were having their wages paid through the Coronavirus Job Retention Scheme, with another 146,000 self-employed workers benefitting from the self-employed grant scheme (see tinyurl.com/3nzcmutp).

Yet, later that year *The Times* (25-10-20) reported that many people in Scotland believed it was a Holyrood scheme:

> Ministers have been shocked by polling evidence that the UK government has had no credit for the coronavirus furlough scheme, which Scottish voters believe is a Scottish government programme.
> tinyurl.com/j95kwr3r

Perhaps that's not surprising!

If you went onto the HMRC website for its Self-Employment Income Support Scheme and followed the process to claim the money – there was absolutely no mention (other than the acronym "HMRC", and the address "gov.uk") that the money was coming courtesy of the British Treasury, and was being brought to Scotland as a consequence of the pooling and sharing of our resources thanks to Scotland being part of the UK.

The word "British" didn't even appear anywhere! Yet this would have been easy to emphasise!

It was a perfect opportunity to help promote the value and benefits of the Union, but it wasn't done, and now we have people in Scotland who think the furlough money was coming from the SNP.

Second Case in point: During August 2022, HMRC sent out huge numbers of personally-addressed letters to Scotland. They were informing people on low incomes that they were to receive a £650 "Cost of Living Payment" by the end of the year.

Yet there was no indication that this money was coming to such economically vulnerable people – who are also voters – from the British Government.

There was no indication (other than the web address "gov.uk") that this was coming to us as a result of being part of the United Kingdom.

The letter mentions the phrase "Government support" twice, and "the Government", but it didn't clarify that it was **the**

British Government. Therefore, many people would just presume it was "the Scottish Government" – as a result of the confusing "Scotland's two governments" rhetoric (chapter 11).

Many people who received this direct and *personally-addressed* communication – who are exactly the sort of people who need to be persuaded of the benefits of the Union – would not have understood that it was the UK "to thank".

Many people would just presume – again – that the money was coming from "the Scottish Government", and from the SNP. This is especially so now that taxes have been complicated by a separate HMRC "Scottish tax rate".

There really is no excuse for continually missing this opportunity!

Imagine if this money had actually come from "the Scottish Government".

There is no doubt that the letter itself would be branded with a blue and white Saltire through its entire length. There would be plenty of references to "the Scottish Government" and its largesse, for which we would be encouraged to give thanks.

There might even be a big picture of the SNP leader in the corner, with a speech bubble saying "The Scottish Government is happy to help you in these difficult times." We are not joking!

THE LESSON

It's important to clearly brand where the money is coming from.

In that regard, all HMRC communications – hard copy and online – require a complete overhaul as a matter of urgency. Dropping a few hints would help; anything to underline and remind us of the importance of the UK in all of this.

For example, let's design the HMRC web pages, and hard-copy letters, so they are branded with British iconography. How about a red, white and blue design? A Union Jack in the corner would be nice! A small thing that would make a big impact.

How about mentioning the "British Government" and "British Treasury" and referring to the eligible "British citizens".

If the Government is giving away billions to British citizens, but is too shy to call it a British project, or to brand it with our national flag, then it is no wonder that the SNP – who know how to do all these things, *all the time* – is winning elections.

Re-brand HMRC online and physical communications British! That's another easy win, which is entirely within any UK Government's ability to deliver very quickly.

3. STOP the BRITISH CIVIL SERVICE PROMOTING the INDY AGENDA

As we explain in the next chapter, the role of the British Civil Service in Scotland is to help the SNP and Greens run the country, not break-up the country.

The present rules which allow civil servants to help "their Ministers" pursue their policy objectives were not put together in the expectation that "their Ministers" would be working to break up the central British State itself!

They are a direct consequence of the upside-down "devolution settlement" which dictates that everything not written down as reserved is presumed to be devolved (see chapter 5).

This anomaly has never been corrected.

We are now at a point where pro-UK people in Scotland are struggling to promote our positive message of unity and solidarity in the face of the combined forces of the British Civil Service, who are being paid by us, to work against us.

The situation is absurd!

It means that pro-UK groups like A Force For Good simply cannot compete with this level of British Taxpayer-funded, anti-UK propaganda. It's well past time to sort it out!

Thankfully, it can be easily fixed.

We need a law to prohibit any part of Her Majesty's Home Civil Service from having any role in any activity which acts against the integrity of the United Kingdom – defined as the maintenance of the UK as a Unitary State and One Nation.

We've detailed the law in the next chapter.

And finally...

A BRITISH DAY BANK HOLIDAY

Let's always be looking for ways to promote Britain and Britishness, socially, culturally, and educationally.

How about a British Day Bank Holiday on the Friday or Monday of the official Birthday Weekend of the King. The Official Birthday falls on the second Saturday in June. It has been celebrated in June since 1908 when Edward VII (born on 9 Nov) moved the ceremony in the hope of good weather.

A Bank Holiday on that weekend would spread out the sense of Britishness – from the official Trooping the Colour event in London – to the country, enabling everyone to share in the event.

It is the perfect date which fits the requirements of being contemporary, relevant to all the UK, an upbeat and happy occasion, in the summer so we can enjoy the weather; and avoids historic, constitutional, or military matters over which there might be disagreement and which don't strike the right tone.

Westminster can still make the law for all parts of the UK, and it must do so here, otherwise the SNP and Greens will do everything they can to prevent it happening in Scotland. The precedents include 5 June 2012, the UK-wide Diamond Jubilee Bank Holiday; 3 June 2022, the UK-wide Platinum

Jubilee Bank Holiday; and 8 May 2023, the UK-wide Coronation Bank Holiday.

This may seem like a little thing in the grand scheme of things, but it is all the little things that the British Government is not doing, or not encouraging, which creates the big problem of separatism and which allows it to dominate.

We have over 100 of these ideas detailed in our 40-page magazine, *Do More Together* available at aforceforgood.uk/shop-1

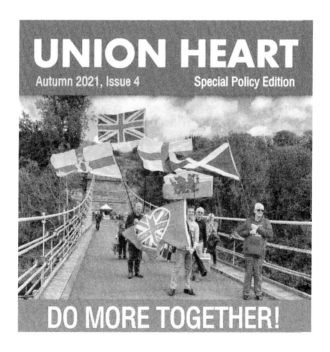

CHAPTER 13

STOP BEING IMPARTIAL, START BEING INVOLVED

The role of the British Civil Service in Scotland is to help the SNP run the country, not break-up the country. Here's the law to fix that!

Too often, the Civil Service is allowed to help the SNP promote matters outside its devolved remit – matters which are properly reserved; or create publications and propaganda for separation; or interfere on matters, at home and abroad, which are legally reserved to the British Parliament – and all of which, we're paying for!

We need a law to prohibit any part of Her Majesty's Home Civil Service from having any role in any activity which acts against the integrity of the United Kingdom.

THE BACKGROUND

The matter of UK Taxpayers' money being spent on SNP projects intended to break up Britain, has been on-going since the SNP took power in May 2007.

Simon Case, the Cabinet Secretary, and head of the Civil Service, appeared before the House of Lords Constitution Committee on 18 July 2023. (1) He responded to Lord Keen's questions as follows (**our emphases**):

> **Lord Keen of Elie:** Why is it only now that we are addressing the question of further guidance for civil servants in Scotland?
>
> **Simon Case:** Because specific instances have arisen that need looking at. We thought that the guidance was clear, but we have had reason to look at various instances and uses of money, so we are looking at it now.
>
> **Lord Keen of Elie:** Yes, but, as you say, it goes back to 2014 at least. **We have had instances of so-called embassies being set up abroad. We have had instances of policies being pursued with regard to independence and, therefore, within the area of reserved matters.** Why is it, as I reiterate, only now that the question of further guidance is being addressed? Why was it not addressed years ago?

Simon Case: I cannot answer for years ago. I assume that it is because predecessors thought the guidance that was there was adequate. It has been brought to my attention in a number of instances now, so I am now discussing with Ministers the propriety and ethics of it. Indeed, if necessary, I will consult with the Civil Service Commission about it, because, to come back to **the rather important point that flows through all this, we all want to protect the integrity and impartiality of our Civil Service.** That is why I want to make sure that civil servants operating in Scotland have very clear guidance about what they can and cannot do, because they deserve, and the whole Civil Service requires them to have, that protection and guidance.

Lord Keen of Elie: The Permanent Secretary and civil servants in Scotland need to know when they are still operating within the requirements of the Civil Service Code.

Simon Case: They certainly do, and they want to. To be clear, I believe that they have been looking at these edge cases diligently, but, as I say, **I want to go back around them all with colleagues in Scotland and with Ministers to make sure that we are doing absolutely what**

we should to protect and preserve that impartiality.

WHAT IS THE LAW?
When the First Minister claims that the promotion of separatist propaganda by the Civil Service is within his "jurisdiction" – within his legal power to require these actions – then he is quite correct.

The Civil Service Code requires Civil Servants to follow the instructions of "their Ministers". This Code was established before anyone ever thought that the "Ministers" would be people who wanted to destroy the United Kingdom itself.

THE ISSUES at STAKE: WHAT WE OPPOSE and WHY
It is important to clarify that we are not complaining about the Civil Service promoting SNP policies which are necessary for the day-to-day running of Scotland. That is a necessary function.

What we oppose, firstly, is UK Taxpayers' money being used to promote the deliberate break-up of the UK. For example, this includes money which is used to develop research, promote literature and videos, and organise events both foreign and domestic, all of which are intended to promote separatism.

Secondly, we oppose this expenditure when the matter of the Constitution – including the Union – and matters such as Foreign Affairs, are legally reserved to Westminster; as listed in Schedule 5 of the Scotland Act 1998.

That is, we oppose it on **the moral principle** that UK Taxpayers' money should not be used to promote the break-up of the UK; on **the economic principle** that UK Taxpayers' money should not be spent into the economy in order to destroy the UK itself; on **the political principle** that this spending is intended to undermine the UK's political structure, and also contradicts the will of the Scottish people as expressed in 2014 to stay in the UK; and on **the legal principle** that such matters are reserved in law to Westminster.

Simon Case is keen to tell us that "the rather important point" is the "impartiality" of the Civil Service in Scotland. If there is impartiality and favouritism for Scottish separatism in the ranks of the Civil Service, then that is a serious matter, but it's not the primary matter. To imagine that "impartiality" is the main issue is to drastically miss the moral, economic, political and legal points!

THIS ANOMALY has NEVER BEEN ADDRESSED
It has never been addressed because the UK Government – to the extent that it was aware – either didn't care; didn't think it was wrong because they thought it was how the "devolution settlement" was meant to work; or because they didn't have the courage to get involved because they didn't have the moral stamina for "the fight".

WHAT HAS TO BE DONE – A NEW LAW

The First Minister is quite correct that – as the law stands – this behaviour is "within his jurisdiction". Therefore, the law needs to be changed! This requires a change to the Civil Service Code, which requires legislation at Westminster. **We've written the new law. Here's what it would look like:**

1. The Home Civil Service (wherever it is based in the UK or worldwide) shall not be used, nor shall it be allowed at any time, to assist or promote by any means, including physical, economic, research, and administrative, any devolved UK administration on any matter which falls outside that administration's devolved competences, or which relates to a reserved matter; especially including but not limited to:

a) The separation of any part of the United Kingdom from the rest of the UK.
b) The promotion, by any means, of policies and activities which are contrary to the UK Government's position on reserved matters.

2. For the avoidance of doubt, it shall also be against the Civil Service Code for any civil servant in Scotland or anywhere in the United Kingdom or worldwide to engage in any activity for a devolved administration which falls outside that administration's devolved competences, or which relates to a reserved matter.

3. It shall be against the Civil Service Code for any civil servant in Scotland or anywhere in the United Kingdom or worldwide to engage in any activity which is aimed at undermining the integrity of the United Kingdom – "integrity" being defined as the maintenance of the UK as a Unitary State and Nation.

4. It shall be against the Civil Service Code for any civil servant in Scotland or anywhere in the United Kingdom or worldwide to participate in the production of a manifesto for a political party, or any publication in any medium which could be construed, or assumed, to resemble or be equivalent to a party political manifesto, such as the "White Paper" of 2013 entitled *Scotland's Future*.

5. The appointment of senior civil servants in Scotland shall be contingent upon them having already served elsewhere in the United Kingdom and also upon them having served in at least one department for the UK Government in Scotland.

6. For the avoidance of doubt, it shall be an option for the UK Government in Scotland to take full control of any department of the Civil Service in Scotland when it is the opinion of the Cabinet Secretary in agreement with the Secretary of State for Scotland, that the department is in contravention of any paragraph or sub-paragraph above.

IT'S TIME to STOP BEING "IMPARTIAL" and START BEING INVOLVED!

We should be cautious when politicians tell us that they want to be "impartial". It can be code for: "To be frank, I'd rather sit on the fence here." It can be code for abdicating responsibility, or staying out of the fight.

The fact is, it's not for the British Government to be "impartial" about the future of the United Kingdom. It is for the British Government to be **highly partial** – to be **highly for** protecting the integrity of the UK.

Does the British Government have the moral stamina to enjoin the fight? Or will it prefer to abdicate responsibility and hide behind the buzz word of "impartiality"?

We hold out faith and hope that we will, someday, have a serious British Government that will speak and act to uphold the integrity of the United Kingdom.

We hold out faith and hope that we will have a responsible British Government that does not use its own people's money to encourage the break-up of the Nation itself.

We hold out faith and hope that we will have a determined British Government that will make it illegal for any separatist administration to spend UK Taxpayers' money on reserved matters, and matters intended to destroy the UK itself.

Is that too much to ask?

As for the SNP and Greens, they can rest assured that they will still be able to promote their pro-separation propaganda. They'll just have to pay for it themselves!

1. UK Parliament pdf at tinyurl.com/5ev3ks92

The British Civil Service helped the SNP campaign for separation by producing the massive *Scotland's Future*. It's an exact anagram of Fraudulent Costs!

PART 5

DEVOLVING OR DISSOLVING?

CHAPTER 14

THE DANGER OF LABOUR'S FEDERALIST PLAN

In December 2022, the Labour Party published its Report, "A New Britain: Renewing our Democracy and Rebuilding our Economy". It was assembled by the former PM Gordon Brown to guide Labour's plans for the 2024 General Election. In the next 3 chapters we examine this plan, we point out its dangers to the continued survival of our Unitary State and One Nation, and we list Rules to Remember for pro-UK politicians dealing with devolution. The page numbers below refer to the pages in the Report.

The Report has 4 premises, which are all debateable. Apparently:

1. Britain is "overcentralised" (p38 and throughout). This is meant to be a fact, despite massive amounts of devolution already.

2. The answer is to devolve even more power.

3. People are said to want this! Apparently, opinion polling by Brown shows people want "more decisions...made locally and regionally, and that local politicians are best placed to understand their needs" (footnote p69). This is questionable!

What's stopping this "close as possible" principle (p70) being extended to everything? For example, some say that "defence" is best reserved at Westminster. SNP supporters would not say that! They want it to be one of those "close" powers.

Anyway, how close is close? In our small group of Islands, everywhere is relatively "close".

Why should decisions and power exercised "closer" be automatically better? The SNP administration has proven itself thoroughly incompetent in building ferries, for example.

Has the context and consequences of more devolution been made clear to the person being polled? For example, if you ask someone, "Do you want more power devolved to Holyrood", they might answer "Yes". If you ask them, "Do you want more power devolved to Holyrood if it would make the break-up of the UK more likely?" then they might answer "No".

4. Devolution is meant to be threatened. Brown believes that the "devolution settlement" is under threat from Westminster (pp102-104), and things must be done to "entrench" (that is, make it very hard to change) devolved power within the British constitution.

This is an exaggeration, and even if it were true, then so what? Not everyone is a supporter of Labour's particular form of "devolution settlement" – whereby everything is presumed to be devolved by default, unless written down as reserved.

What does Labour plan to do about it?

"ENTRENCH the SEWEL CONVENTION in a NEW SECOND CHAMBER"

The Sewell Convention is written into law in Article 2 of the Scotland Act 2016.

It states that "the Parliament of the United Kingdom will not normally legislate with regard to devolved matters without the consent of the Scottish Parliament."

The guideline is that Westminster will not "normally" legislate on any matter which is devolved, without the agreement of Holyrood. This includes over-ruling or over-turning or taking back, any Holyrood bill or law or power, without Holyrood's consent.

It can still do it, of course, and it does.

However, Brown wants to change the "normally" requirement to something which, in effect, will mean virtually *never*!

His way of strengthening this "devolution settlement" and dissuading or preventing Westminster from getting involved in devolved matters, while making it very difficult for Westminster to over-rule, or over-turn devolved bills or laws, or take back devolved powers, is to make the Sewel Convention a "protected constitutional law" (p103).

Labour would do this by **abolishing the House of Lords** and establishing a new elected Second Chamber, made up of representatives from Scotland, Northern Ireland and Wales, and 9 Regions in England.

This new Chamber will "entrench" the Sewell Convention by having the ability to vote on, and potentially reject, any such disputed matters related to devolution (pp140-142).

That is, if a situation similar to the Gender Recognition Reform (GRR) Bill came up again (when the Secretary of State for Scotland prevented this Holyrood Bill from becoming law) then not only the House of Commons, but also the new elected Second Chamber – made up of representatives from all the devolved areas – would have to agree! In the event of a disagreement then it is proposed to make it extremely difficult for the House of Commons to push through the policy (p141).

In other words, the new Second Chamber is going to take upon itself the presumed duty to defend devolution from all attempts to affect it or take back powers.

It doesn't take much imagination to realise that it will quickly turn into a belligerent chamber which exists to prevent the House of Commons touching anything to do with devolution.

Imagine a British Government trying to prevent something like the GRR Bill going through Holyrood again, or if it tried to take back some devolved power.

Imagine if it were a Conservative government in the House of Commons, with a Labour, Lib Dem, Green and SNP majority in the Second Chamber. They would all vote it down simply because they wanted to make life difficult for the Conservatives.

It would also work against Labour if there were a Labour government and the majority in the Second Chamber was anti-Labour.

The Chamber would become a vocal arm for the devolved interests. It would be a recipe for continuous constitutional aggravation and chaos.

"Defending devolution" would become its mantra and it would develop in such a way that it would constantly challenge the power of the House of Commons. It would represent, not pan-UK concerns, but those of "the nations and regions of the UK in a very explicit way." (p145)

Any British Government would be scared away from touching any devolved matter – even ones which negatively impact the integrity of the UK – because it would be too much hassle.

Instead of having to pick a fight with Holyrood, they will have to pick a fight with their own Second Chamber in their own Parliament – and they will just not be bothered!

Labour's plans would create a heavy rod for any government's back.

In its over concern to safeguard devolution, it forgets to safeguard the Unitary State. It will make unitary legislation, for all of the UK, extremely difficult.

It is not a union proposal. It is a federal proposal which could make UK-wide government impossible.

MAINTAIN THE "UNION SAFEGUARDS"

When devolving power, all matters need to be considered from the hard fact that Scotland has a powerful separatist movement that wants to destroy the Union.

Giving power to "the local" can be a problem in areas where a certain party might always tend to dominate in that locality.

For a better balance of power, it's necessary for the central power – in this case, the British Parliament and Government – to also have power in local areas in order to represent those who do not always vote for, or support, the local power.

For example, it is important in a devolved nation like Scotland, where the SNP may continue to dominate at the Holyrood level for quite some time, that there are other sources of power which are able to represent those of us who support the UK.

That's where the power of the centre comes in, and that's why its power must also be protected.

Setting up safeguards to defend devolution means that the safeguards to defend the Union are being forgotten.

There will be times when the centre has to stand up for all those of us who believe in the UK and who want the devolved institution – which may be run by people hostile to the continued existence of the UK – to be restrained where and when appropriate.

To try to set up constitutional barriers to such a Union Safeguard – as Gordon Brown and the Labour Party is planning to do – is to make it easier to destroy the UK.

It is elevating devolution as an end in itself, which could end in the dissolution of the United Kingdom. **The centre must be able to hold!**

Next page: A Stepping Stone to Separation.
A Force For Good distributed these leaflets outside the Labour Party Conference in Dundee on
10 March 2018.

WHAT IS FEDERALISM?

Federalism (or 'Home Rule') makes Holyrood responsible for everything except Defence, Foreign Affairs, Immigration and Financial Regulation. Our pro-UK organisation, *A Force For Good* opposes the Fragmentation of Federalism because:

1. IT WILL NOT STOP SCOTTISH NATIONALISM

Nationalists only care about Independence. Federalism will not stop them trying to Break Up Britain.

2. IT MAKES SEPARATION EASIER

It gives Nationalists more of what they want. It makes it easier for them to say 'nothing much will change and only one more step'. It makes their job easier.

3. IT DESTABILISES THE UNION

It leaves Westminster with all the controversial stuff. It makes it easy for the Nationalists to frame the British Parliament as the perpetual Bad Guy.

4. IT ENDS POOLING/SHARING OF RESOURCES

It breaks the shared British-wide economic community. It damages our social desire to pool our resources with people throughout the UK.

5. IT DAMAGES OUR INDUSTRIAL SINEWS

It corrupts the potential for Britain to build its economic strength and create jobs through shared British-wide research, development and cooperation.

6. IT ENCOURAGES THE NATIONALIST AGENDA

It makes us stare at our Scottish navel and obsess about the divisive Independence agenda, instead of focusing on the Big Picture of Britain, our unity, and shared identity.

7. IT MEANS ENDLESS REFERENDUMS

It gives the Nationalists power to hold another referendum whenever they want. Right now, Westminster can forbid it.

8. IT'S POOR STRATEGY

Only a paper wall separates Federalism from Separation. A political party which advocates 'Federalism' sets itself up as the weaker version of a stronger brand. It hurts itself, and only benefits those who see Federalism as a Stepping Stone towards Separation.

OUR ANSWER: We need Ever Closer Union in our Islands, not the Fragmentation of Federalism. We need *Solidarity not Division*. We need Industry and Jobs not Constitutional Obsession.

ONE BIG COUNTRY

CHAPTER 15

DEVO-RULES TO REMEMBER FOR PRO-UK POLITICIANS

Here are the basic rules to guide pro-UK politicians when dealing with devolution.

Rule Number 1: Devolution is always Dangerous to a Union in the presence of a Separatist Movement
This requires us to be ultra-cautious about devolving any power in a context where the separatist movement will use it against the Union itself.

Rule Number 2: Any Power Devolved *will* be used Against You in ways you must Learn to Foresee
To paraphrase the Duke of Wellington, the business of politics is figuring out what's on the other side of the hill. Take for example, the idea in Brown's Report about "devolving the administration of the job centre network" (p107).

Example: Job Centre Devolution

Consider how this policy – which will convince *no-one* to vote Labour – will end up being disastrous for the Union.

In this case, there is no question that the apparently "trivial" matter of Job Centre devolution would be repurposed by the SNP for very serious and effective political ends.

For example, the SNP would rebrand the Job Centre as "Jobs Scotland". It would emblazon the exteriors and interiors of the buildings with Scottish Government logos, posters and booklets.

It would ensure that all hard-copy and online communications make it very clear that it is "the Scottish Government", and even the SNP, to thank for the money going into your wallet or the new job you've just found!

This will be used to hide the role of the UK Treasury – the British Taxpayers throughout the UK – who are directly funding this welfare provision in the first place. This will erode the psychological sense of solidarity that comes with pooling and sharing our economic resources across the UK.

At the same time, the SNP will deliberately configure "Jobs Scotland" to operate in such a way that it is incompatible with wider UK welfare policy, which the SNP will position as mean-spirited and cruel. It will use this apparent difference as an argument to demand full tax-raising powers, and, of course, separation. **That is, the only consequences of Job Centre devolution will be:**

a) Tens of thousands of Scots will have been psychologically distanced from the UK.
b) Politically, the SNP will accuse the British Parliament of "denying" the freedom of "Jobs Scotland" to administer the SNP's "much more kindly and generous" welfare policies.
c) Most people will not understand why something called "Jobs Scotland" is not free to set its own policies anyway? They will buy into the SNP's talking points that this is some kind of "oppressive colonial control", and it is the Union which is bad.
d) The pooling and sharing of British Taxpayers' money to fund welfare provision throughout the UK is an easily-understood demonstration of British economic solidarity, and a powerful argument for the Union, yet this fact will now be hidden by the term "Jobs Scotland", and it will have been completely removed from the political discussion.
e) Absolutely no-one will have been turned away from separatism.
f) More people will have been encouraged to look to Holyrood as the solution, and the separatist position will have been strengthened.
g) The Labour Party, which introduced this power, will lose out *once again* to the SNP.

All of the above *will* happen, as night follows day – because this is what inevitably happens when you give more powers to a separatist administration that opposes you.

Rule Number 3: Do not Abandon People to the Devolved Power

The Union Safeguards must be maintained. The central British Parliament will always have a relevant and important role and must maintain its ability to deliver.

That's especially important when those in charge in the devolved area are elected by a minority of the electorate. In Scotland, for example, the combined vote for the SNP, Greens and 3 small pro-separation parties in the 2021 Holyrood election averaged out at only 31.4% of the entire electorate – see our article at tinyurl.com/223h4ph9

What about the democratic mandate of the over two thirds of the Scottish electorate who did not vote for separation? What about protecting our mandate!

And what about the concerns and interests of everyone in the rest of the United Kingdom? Remember, we're all involved here! Our democratic rights and political beliefs need protecting too. We want to see UK-wide policies enacted in Scotland too.

It is the job of the Union Parliament to do just that and it must not abdicate its role.

Rule Number 4: There is No Voter who is solely an Enthusiast for Devolution, and so don't make Concessions to this Imaginary Demographic

The Labour Party's error is to assume that there is a demographic of Scots who can be lured away from separatism by devolution reform. Let's be realistic. There is nobody like this! Indeed, Gordon Brown is probably the most enthusiastic person *in the entire UK* for devolution. He imagines everyone is like him; that we're all fascinated with the obscure technicalities of public sector policy.

The reality is that in post-2014 Scotland, most people see devolution as either:

1. A means to separation – a useful device to manipulate loyalties, frame narratives of oppression, and manufacture grievances.
2. A tolerated convenience – these are people in the middle who might favour, or don't mind, some sort of devolution *within* the UK, but they're not emotional about it and they don't bother themselves with the details.
3. An annoyance – these people see it as a liability, more trouble than it is worth, and often they want less!

If you want to keep the UK together then you have to appeal to the political interests of demographics 2 and 3, and against the political interests of those who want to break up the UK.

The fact that UK policy makers must grasp – and especially the Labour Party – is that there is no substantial demographic of people in Scotland whose feelings about devolution are so technically-based, that they will turn to separatism if they don't get more devolution.

Similarly, there is no substantial demographic that can be lured away from voting for the SNP by an assortment of arbitrary, but always dangerous, concessions.

Example: "Entrenching the Sewell Convention"
As we examined in the previous chapter, does Labour imagine that the nationalists are going to say, "Yippee, the Sewel Convention is entrenched in a reformed Second Chamber? Now we don't need independence!"

Chances are they won't even know about it, much less understand what's happened if it were explained to them.

So it doesn't seem as if Labour has thought any of this through!

It's as if Brown's Report has been written in a fantasy world where there will be a perpetual Labour Government in the House of Commons, a perpetual Labour majority in the new Second Chamber, and the devolved nations and regions will all be run by agreeable Labour administrations!

Rule Number 5: Do not Build a Rod for Your Back
Devolution has a way of coming back to bite you. Case in point: By the time of the next Holyrood election in 2026, the Labour Party in Scotland will have been out of power for 19 years!

The bottom line is that all proposals for "self-government" for the "nations and regions" need to take into account the extent to which such proposals might enable and strengthen those who want to break up the UK. All proposals need to be thought through from that angle.

There is a very real danger that too much "self-government" will only dissolve the shared bonds entirely.

The Labour Party's report does not show any understanding of that political reality, or the likely consequences of what is proposed.

This is especially the case in the proposal to abolish the House of Lords and replace it with an "Assembly of the Nations and Regions – as we further examine in the next chapter.

Oh, and the final rule...

Rule Number 6: Separatism cannot ever be Satisfied by Devolution

Our knowledge has been forged on the Streets of Scotland with the help of our fantastic AFFG Table Team, here in Glasgow, 20-5-23.

CHAPTER 16

"ASSEMBLY OF THE NATIONS AND REGIONS" 11 REASONS WHY IT'S A BAD IDEA FOR THE UK

The Labour Party's plan to abolish the House of Lords and establish an "Assembly of the Nations and Regions" will turn the Second Chamber into a squabbling shop which will give the separatist voice a new platform at the heart of the British Parliament, undermine the UK, and damage a Labour Government.

1- It will prevent UK-wide legislation.
Whether the House of Lords needs reform is an important question. From a pro-UK perspective, the first thing we ask is: How would reform affect the politics of the Union, and ultimately, the integrity of the United Kingdom itself?

In chapter 14 we examined Labour's plans to "entrench the Sewell Convention" by abolishing the House of Lords and setting up a new Second Chamber called an "Assembly of the Nations and Regions", made up of elected representatives from the 3 devolved nations and 9 regions in England.

The Chamber would be specially-tasked with protecting the Sewell Convention which states that Westminster cannot "normally" legislate on any matter which is devolved. This would include debating and voting on any attempt by the UK Government of the day to over-rule or over-turn or take back, any Holyrood bill or law or power, without Holyrood's consent.

If a situation similar to the Gender Recognition Reform Bill were to arise again, then the UK Government could only prevent it happening if it received the agreement of the new Second Chamber. If it didn't receive agreement, then it would be made constitutionally very difficult for it to push through the policy.

It seems inevitable that finding agreement with representatives elected from the *devolved* nations and regions – who are going to inevitably take upon themselves the perceived duty to defend devolution – is going to be virtually impossible. So much so that no UK Government is going to bother touching any devolved matter for fear of the fight that will ensue!

In effect, by abolishing the House of Lords and replacing it with a Chamber made up of representatives elected specifically upon devolved matters, Labour will have changed the "normally", in the Sewell Convention, to "never"!

Here's another 10 reasons why this is bad for the Union and bad for the Labour Party.

2- It's turning the Second Chamber from pan-UK to nationalistic.

Putting aside whether the House of Lords needs reform, there is one good thing about the House of Lords at present: It is *not* associated with any particular part of the UK. It represents it as a unity.

We're calling this element of its character, "pan-UK".

That is, the Lords do not conduct their business by thinking of the UK in a fragmented way – as England v Northern Ireland v Scotland v Wales. At present, the Second Chamber is a pan-UK chamber which thinks first and foremost of the UK, rather than competing parts. In that sense it can be considered to be a quietly "unionist" chamber.

Gordon Brown's Report says that "the present House of Lords...does not look at issues from the perspective of the nations and regions of the UK." (p139) He says it as if that's a bad thing. However, that's a strength.

The Lords are appointed, and don't claim to speak for any particular area of the UK, although each may have his or her own local interests. They come from all over, and they don't make a thing about their political Scottishness or Englishness or otherwise. They examine policies for all the UK.

That is, **the House of Lords avoids platforming the separatist voice**, and it avoids nationalistic arguments. Indeed, the SNP boycotts the Chamber!

What these Labour Party plans intend to do is up-end that pan-UK approach, and have the Chamber, in Brown's words, "represent the nations and regions of the UK in a very explicit way." (p145)

They will change something which is nominally, modestly, quietly unionist – in the sense of representing all of the UK without making a thing about it – to something which is explicitly nationalistic.

They will change it to something which is explicitly divided into Scotland, Wales, Northern Ireland, and English Regions.

How on earth will that help keep the UK together? That just risks descending into a separatist squabbling shop.

The "Assembly of the Nations and Regions" risks becoming a constitutional calamity, a vocal and angry "Separatist Senate" where politicians are going to see political gain in standing up and shouting for their particular nations and regions, against each other, and especially against the House of Commons, and the Government of the day.

How will that help Labour?

3- Abolition of the House of Lords is not answering a strong demand.

The House of Lords may or may not need reform, but there is no big political demographic whose priority is to abolish the House of Lords. It's an obscure policy which is unlikely to come up "on the doorstep".

4- Where is the political demand for entrenching constitutional matters like the Sewel Convention?

The number of people who vote SNP but could be persuaded to return to Labour if they thought that there were some kind of constitutional safeguard against Holyrood laws being overturned, must be very small.

5- Very few people are genuinely worried about devolution being overturned.

It's addressing a concern that is only heard from SNP politicians and commentators.

Indeed, the Gender Recognition Reform Bill – which was prevented from passing by the UK Government in 2023 – showed that many people in Scotland, including SNP supporters, were very happy when Westminster stepped in and stopped it.

6- There are people in Scotland who want Holyrood decisions overturned more often.

There are many people in Scotland who want Westminster to be able to stop certain bills being presented at Holyrood, and to stop certain laws being passed, and to take back powers when necessary. Why alienate them?

7- It is making a rod for the UK government's back, including a Labour government's back!

What happens if a Labour government wants to prevent an SNP bill, or overturn an SNP law, and tries to do so? It will be virtually impossible. It will be hung by its own petard. It will be beaten by the very system it set up!

8- It gives the SNP another platform.

At present, there are no SNP Lords. That is, Scottish separatism does not have a voice in the Second Chamber. The SNP has chosen to absent itself. That is, at least, one good thing from a unionist perspective.

Yet Brown proposes to change this in order that a second chamber "should represent the nations and regions of the UK in a very explicit way." (p145) This will, of course, lead to the entrance into the Second Chamber of a substantial number of people who are opposed to the UK's very existence.

It will give them a platform which they do not currently possess. Labour will (once again) be building a platform for its opponents!

9- It will only grandstand controversial issues related to devolution.

The Chamber will manufacture controversy where none need exist. It will create fights which could have been avoided. This will be to the detriment of the Union, and ultimately of the United Kingdom.

10- The Labour Party will suffer, and the SNP will be rejuvenated just as it begins to fail.

It will put some pro-UK people off voting Labour, and just as Brown's "Vow" and the political dynamic which followed, helped the SNP to bounce back after they lost in 2014, so Brown's "Assembly" idea looks like it could give the SNP a new lease of life, just as it struggles for relevance.

11- The SNP will not thank you.

They will continue to misrepresent the reality of the British Constitution to their supporters, as they always do.

So what is going on here?

LABOUR is TRYING to MOVE THE UK to a FEDERAL STRUCTURE

Federalism is not Unionism. It's a slippery slope to separation.

Labour is taking a cavalier attitude towards the integrity of the Union. There seems no sense that when you give away powers, and entrench these powers, then the centre – the Union Parliament itself – will struggle to hold.

There seems to be an unspoken notion that if you only devolve enough powers, then the separatist demand in Scotland will somehow go away. However, the Scottish nationalist dynamic is a far more complicated matter, which has many motivations – virtually none of which are appeased by devolution, as per Rule Number 6 in chapter 15!

If that had been the case, then devolution would have "killed nationalism stone dead", as stated by George Robertson, one of Gordon Brown's Labour Party colleagues back in 1995.

It's well past time to learn that lesson!

IT'S TIME to RESPECT the UNION MANDATE and the UNION SETTLEMENT

The deeper issue which gives rise to this attitude is that there is no respect here for the Union Mandates. That is, the fact that the British Parliament has constitutional, democratic and popular mandates to govern for all of the UK and to keep it together; mandates given to it by everyone who votes at the General Election.

The Report speaks as if these Union Mandates do not exist or have not even been thought about. It is as if the only "mandate" which is to be respected is whatever one the separatists are shouting about.

Everything is seen from the point of view of the noisy nationalists.

Well, how about respecting the majority of people in Scotland who don't want the Union to break up. How about a Respect Agenda for us.

It's time to make our Union safer and stronger. It's time to talk about the Union Settlement!

This is volume 1 of an annual series which together will create A Big Book for the Union. If you like what you've read, please encourage others to purchase a copy, or gift copies to friends, politicians, opinion formers, and libraries. You can find A Wee Book for the Union at aforceforgood.uk/shop-1

PART 6

ABOUT A FORCE FOR GOOD

CHAPTER 17

THE PRINCIPLES UPON WHICH WE STAND

A Force For Good was established on 21 March 2012. We have become Scotland's best-known and most colourful pro-UK campaign group and think tank.

We have a clear, well thought through, philosophy of Union which represents the Position upon which we stand, and from which we judge the Philosophy, Policy, Projects and Activity which we promote.

We've distilled it into our **4-point Position Statement**. These 4 fundamental Principles also describe the Territory, the Nature, the Purpose, and the Form of Government of our United Kingdom.

1. The United Kingdom of Great Britain and Northern Ireland shall be maintained.

This is our Territory.

2. The United Kingdom is, and shall remain, primarily a Unitary State and One Nation.

[*"A unitary state is a sovereign state governed as a single entity in which the central government is the supreme authority." (Wikipedia)*]

This is our Nature.

We are not merely a "union of nations". We are primarily and predominantly a **Nation of Unions**. We are not merely a "family of nations". We are a **Nation of Families**.

That's important because if we conceive of the United Kingdom only as a "union of nations" then we are thinking of our relationship in an unstable way. We are opening the door to forms of destabilising devolution which do not properly take into account our Unitary Nature; which do not properly take into account the fact that we are **One Big Country**.

Political attitudes which do not properly comprehend the Unitary Nature of the United Kingdom will grease the slippery slope towards forms of destabilising federalism, slow independence and, ultimately, separation.

3. Ever Closer Union between all the people and parts of the United Kingdom shall be pursued: including but not limited to elements; social, cultural, educational, economic, legal, territorial and political.

This is our Purpose.

4. The United Kingdom is a Constitutional Monarchy and Representative Parliamentary Democracy; and the House of Windsor shall continue to provide the Head of State.

This is our Form of Government.

We are a Constitutional Monarchy where the King is the Head of State, and where the ultimate authority to make and pass legislation rests with the British Parliament, and the People who elect it.

We recognise the importance of that Form of Government in conferring upon our Islands our unique character and identity.

Our NATION OF UNIONS and NATION OF FAMILIES

We know the roots of the United Kingdom go far beyond the Parliamentary Union of 1707, or the Regal Union of the Crowns of 1603, but stretch far back into the dawn of time.

It is that understanding which informs our work.

We have a Narrative – an overall Story – within which we understand ourselves and make our case.

It is a Union Story, and it goes right back to the dawn of time.

Discovering and telling this story has been the work of A Force For Good since we established on 21 March 2012.

It begins, to quote the words of the song:

***When Britain First, At Heaven's Command
Arose from out the Azure Main***
*This was the Charter of the Land
And Guardian Angels Sang this Strain
Rule Britannia, Britannia Rule the Waves
Britons Never, Never, Never Shall be Slaves.*

That was written by the Scotsman James Thomson, who had the same attitude towards Britain as we do.

We believe that since Britain first came out the sea and began to be populated, it has been on a journey tending towards Union; towards ever closer and greater Union. Sometimes suffering setbacks, but generally moving through time, towards Union – with our participation and help.

So that's where we're coming from!

We develop these points every day across our Social Media platforms, on our Website, in hard-copy publications, and in the Streets. We use them as the basis to develop Strategies and Policies necessary to strengthen our United Kingdom.

The passage of time should be bringing us closer. It should not be driving us further apart!

If you agree, then read on to find out how you can get involved in this Great Work of Time.

Next page: A Force For Good's Coronation Day Celebration, George Square, Glasgow, 6-5-23.

CHAPTER 18

OUR AIMS

1. Maintain the British Union
We promote the value and benefits of Britain so that people will want to keep it together.

2. Keep Scotland British
We educate about our shared heritage and we defend it. We stand by our ancestors and our national institutions. We help people appreciate and celebrate the vast inheritance which we enjoy today. We promote the value of the British identity, and we help people to be proud to be both Scottish and British.

3. Raise the Level of Pro-UK Support
We aim to raise the numbers of people who love the UK and who want us to stay together. In

Scotland, we aim to raise the percentage of people who support the UK from 55% to 65% for starters.

4. Defeat the Separatist Political Position
We work to defeat the false arguments of the nationalists, to expose their failure at Holyrood, and to oppose further devolution and federalism which are dangerous Stepping Stones to Separation.

HOW WE ACHIEVE OUR AIMS
We achieve our Aims by **communicating** our Philosophy and Policy through our Online Platforms, through our Printed Advocacy, and through our Physical Activism. For example, we:

1. Tell the British Story – Recall to Memory our National Inheritance
Each day, across all our platforms, we provide the context to our pro-UK position – the Who, What, When, Where and Why! We remember the past, to explain the present, to help move with hope into the future.

We show where we've been, so we know where we are, so we know where we should be going.

In so doing, we educate, inspire, and encourage people to see the value and benefits of the United Kingdom, the advantage of being British, and the importance of Scotland in the UK.

This is especially important at a time when others seek not only to forget the past, but to actively destroy it. By so doing, we:

2. Create Intellectual Protection for the British Identity in Scotland

We do this by educating around British history and identity, constitution and politics. Practical ways that we deliver this is through publishing daily on our Social Media platforms, on our Website, and through regular printed literature, including our magazine *Union Heart*, which is distributed free on our Street Stalls, and to monthly donors who request copies.

3. Turn Scotland Red, White and Blue

We increase the visibility of Britishness and its colourful symbolism in Scotland, via our amazing Street Activism, including our "Counter-Presence" events when the Scottish nationalists hold their marches; and at our Street Stalls where we fly the flag for the UK and distribute our material.

4. Expose the Scottish Nationalist Marches

We are famous for delivering video footage, and precise counts, of the exaggerated "Separatist Shuffles". We do this to expose their lies in order that we are not misled and demoralised by their false claims, and to ensure that we have a strategic understanding of their true strength and current state of support.

5. Promote the UK as a Force For Good in the World

Our national vision – communicated on our platforms – is about service to humanity, not "freedom" from the English! Together, we have a destiny to benefit the world.

WHAT WILL HAPPEN in 2024 and 2026?

The General Election is in 2024 and the Holyrood Election is scheduled for 7 May 2026. The SNP/Greens – and their allies in the media – will use every minute to seed disaffection, to destabilise the UK, and to culturally attack Britishness. What might happen in 2024-26? Here are 4 possible outcomes:

1. Conservative Win

If the Conservatives win, but the SNP performs well, then it will misrepresent its vote as a "mandate" for a referendum. The SNP will campaign for this in the run-up to the 2026 election. If the SNP/Greens win that again, then whether the British Government would grant one depends on who is Prime Minister and his or her ability to stand up for the UK.

2. Labour Win, or Labour/LibDem Coalition

Similarly, if the SNP perform well in 2024 then there is a possibility that a referendum could be granted under pressure from Labour or Lib Dem MPs. This would not happen until after a 2026 Holyrood election, if it was won by the SNP/Greens.

3. Tory/Lib Dem Coalition
The Lib Dems could pressure the Tories to grant a referendum after a 2026 Holyrood election which was won by the SNP/Greens.

4. Labour/SNP Coalition
The SNP would enter coalition with Labour on the basis that a second referendum is to be granted.

The threat of a second referendum is not going away. It could become a real thing very fast. Therefore, we must prepare!

OUR 5-YEAR PRIORITIES for A FORCE FOR GOOD
1. Keep going!

2. Get bigger – measured by more email sign-ups, more donors, more activists, and greater online reach. It is absolutely essential for us to continue to grow the reach of our Online Platforms, expand our Video and Audio capabilities, and build our ability to mobilise for Action.

3. Get more effective – produce more physical, printed and online material, and outdoor events, which help people to appreciate the United

Kingdom, make the case for it, and win the arguments.

Our approach at A Force For Good is to stand on the rock of principle, and hold fast. This ensures the waves of "the latest thing" pass over us. We won't ride them, but that means we won't get drowned by them either.

That's why we're still here, after all these years. If you like our attitude, please help us. The next chapter explains how.

A Force For Good flying the flags at our Counter Presence on the Royal Mile, 5-10-19, when we counted 11,286 of the Separatist Shufflers, and not the "200,000" that the march organisers pretended, or the "250,000" that an SNP MP hallucinated!

CHAPTER 19

HOW YOU CAN BE INVOLVED

A Force For Good moves forward safe in the knowledge that in the years since we began this work on 21 March 2012, we have built a committed, skilled and professional production Team, a group of wonderful activists, and many kind donors who love our **One Big Country** and who are determined to keep it together!

If you'd like to be part of this work, then please consider how you are best placed to help. Here are things you can do.

1. KEEP IN TOUCH
a. Sign Up to Stay in Touch with a fortnightly Email Update at aforceforgood.uk/sign-up

b. Follow us on our Social Media platforms.

This really helps! Our main platforms are:

Facebook.com/UKaForceForGood
Instagram.com/UKaForceForGood
Twitter.com/UKaForceForGood
YouTube.com/UKaForceForGood
TikTok.com/@UKaForceForGood
Substack.com/@UKaForceForGood

We also have a modest presence on:
Patreon.com/UKaForceForGood
Bitchute.com/UKaForceForGood
Rumble.com/UKaForceForGood
Odysee.com/@UKaForceForGood

c. Email us at *contact@aforceforgood.uk* if you want to join our Street Activism, or if you have special skills which might be of assistance.

2. PROMOTE OUR WORK
i. It's easy to spread the message on Social Media. Please share our posts from all our platforms.
ii. Copy the URL of our articles on our Website at **aforceforgood.uk** and our videos on YouTube, and our podcasts, and share them via email and social media. (Also see our previous Legacy Site at http://www.aforceforgood.org.uk Please note the Legacy Site is "http" and not "https" meaning that if you use the latter protocol, then it won't work.)
iii. Share our podcasts:

- Good Evening Britain (2022 onwards) is at aforceforgood.uk/podcast-2
- Good Morning UK. Have Your Say (2021) is at aforceforgood.uk/podcast-1
- Saturday Street Stall (2020) is at aforceforgood.uk/podcast

iv. Feel free to print-out our articles and send them to MPs, MSPs and Opinion Formers.

v. Invite Friends to follow us on Facebook: Use the "Invite friends" button (under the 3 little dots on a browser or mobile). Click on it and scroll through your Friends. A message will be sent to those you select saying "[Your Name] invited you to like A Force For Good". It's an easy way to help the Union!

3. PURCHASE OUR PRO-UK MERCHANDISE

- Our badges, flags, books, mags and more are at aforceforgood.uk/shop-1

- Our T-shirt and Hoodie Store is at a-force-for-good.creator-spring.com

- Buy extra copies of this book and send them to friends, politicians, and opinion-formers.

4. KEEP OUR MOTOR RUNNING!

We understand that some people don't want to be physically active for personal or job-related reasons. If that's you, then here's a way you can help those of us who *are* able to be active.

a. Monthly Support: We depend upon our monthly Union Supporters. These are the fantastic people who give from £0.69p a week (£3 a month) at **aforceforgood.uk/union-supporters** or via the GoCardless and PayPal links at that page.
b. One-Off Support: Please chip-in when the spirit moves you at aforceforgood.uk/donate2
or via the GoCardless or PayPal links above.
c. Set up a Standing Order to AFFG Productions Ltd, RBS, 10816660, 832108.
d. Or send a Cheque payable to
"AFFG Productions Ltd" at A Force For Good, Clyde Offices, 48 West George Street, Glasgow, G2 1BP.
e. Support us with Super Chats and Super Thanks on YouTube.
f. Become a paid subscriber on our Substack.
g. Donate to our Yule Britannia Christmas Crowdfunder.co.uk every December.
h. Please consider buying extra copies of this book to send to friends, politicians, and opinion-formers.
i. Ask your local Library to order a copy, or even donate one.

5. TELL OTHERS ABOUT AFFG

Next time you hear someone complaining about the state of the nation, please point them in our direction, and suggest that they donate to A Force For Good. After all, there is no point in complaining if they don't intend to do anything.

After many years in the ring, we've proven our worth! Our close-knit AFFG Team has the experience, and is ideally placed to take this work forward. With your help we will continue!

Believe us when we say, the men and women of A Force For Good will stay the course for the Union we so love!

6. FIGHT ON AFTER YOU'VE GONE!

The United Kingdom is the Great Work of Time and you can help A Force For Good fight for our One Big Country even after you die, by leaving something in your Will.

All you need to do is say that you're leaving a fixed sum of money, or a particular item, or a portion of your estate to "AFFG Productions Ltd at Clyde Offices, 48 West George Street, Glasgow, G2 1BP, Company number 533791".

If you have already written your Will then you can contact your Lawyer to add this.

You can Keep Standing for Great Britain… from the Great Beyond!

A Force For Good's Counter Presence on the Royal Mile, 6-10-18.

Printed in Great Britain
by Amazon